26

26

A Behind-the-Scenes Tour of Life with Cerebral Palsy

Stuart Maloney

authorHOUSE®

AuthorHouse™
1663 Liberty Drive
Bloomington, IN 47403
www.authorhouse.com
Phone: 1-800-839-8640

First published by AuthorHouse   10/14/2011

ISBN: 978-1-4670-0788-7 (sc)
ISBN: 978-1-4670-0789-4 (ebk)

Printed in the United States of America

Any people depicted in stock imagery provided by Thinkstock are models, and such images are being used for illustrative purposes only.
Certain stock imagery © Thinkstock.

This book is printed on acid-free paper.

CONTENTS

DEDICATED TO MUM, SIMONE, CHARLES, AND
RACH

IN LOVING MEMORY OF DAD

FOREWORD BY JAMES FAIRBRASS

What does one say in a foreword? One could lament about times shared, celebrate struggles overcome, or reveal a shared history between the book's author and the writer of this sometimes-brief introductory statement. Perhaps it becomes a love letter to a great writer who is sadly no longer with us. Possibilities abound.

Look in a dictionary and you'll find something like this: fore·word *noun* a short introductory statement in a published work, as a book, especially when written by someone other than the author.

So with the above definition as my starting point, I set off on an epic journey (a journey that didn't actually require leaving the sofa) to write the best possible foreword about one of the most amazing people I know—and someone who I have the pleasure of calling my brother.

I've known Stuart Maloney since I was four years old.

That's twenty-five years ago. I'm getting old.

He is part of my family. Not the 'blood is thicker than water', 'love them because you have to' type family. Stuart is part of the family that I choose to have, one of the few people that, over a great many years and some serious ups and downs, have been a constant in my life—and for that I feel truly blessed.

Loving. Kind. Compassionate. Loyal. Fiercely determined. Positive. Hilarious. Generous. Smart. Grateful. I could keep going with this list, but I think you get the idea. If the world had thrown half the problems in my direction that has been flung at Stu, I'd be a mess, completely buried by all of the issues and tangled by all the complications.

How he's managed to keep going over the years is beyond me. I can't say I wouldn't have quit. And it's not just getting by or making do. He's living a life to be proud of—that anyone should be proud of, disabled or not. He has been, and continues to be, a constant inspiration to me.

We don't see each other often nowadays. It was six years between our most recent visits. But distance doesn't matter and neither does how often we talk. Regardless of how long it's been, it's like no time has passed at all. Sure the little details change—job, home, mobile number—but really, it's always the same.

It might sound as if I take this for granted, and in the past that may have been true. Youth really is embarrassing at times. But I now realize what I have. I know that it's a rare thing, something that should be protected and taken care of.

I love you, brother.
J.

FOREWORD BY BRADLEY FAIRBRASS

I've known Stuart for longer than I haven't known him. We're not related by blood, but by any other measure of what family is: the people you want support from when times are hard, those you want to share the good times with, and the ones you know will always be there for you regardless of personal circumstance, geography, or any other obstacle you care to think of. Stuart is my brother.

We met sometime in our first week of Primary School (as it was a while ago, the specifics allude me). It was obvious, even to a four-year-old child, that Stuart was different. His disabilities differentiated him from the rest of my class who, looking back on things now, seem to have morphed into one teary-eyed, snotty-nosed mass. I never saw his differences as being anything else other than a part of him and certainly no reason not to make a new friend.

A certain amount of credit for my open-mindedness has to go to my parents. I was, after all, only four years old, and at that age you don't really have the time to contemplate the grand notions of non-judgementalism and mindfulness when there are Transformers to be played with and balls to be kicked into the next-door neighbour's garden.

While it was Stuart's disabilities that differentiated him from the crowd, I too stood out from our classmates as being different. I have an identical twin brother, so in my case, being different revolved around looking identical to someone else. Maybe that's where our friendship started—our shared experience of being seen as different by our classmates.

When I sat down to write this, I inevitably started to replay a lifetime of memories, trying to find one that epitomised both Stuart as an individual and our friendship.

I remember the excitement I felt as I stood next to Stuart's hospital bed when he proudly proclaimed that the now-empty bed next to him had recently been occupied by Warwick Davis's daughter. He had spoken to *Willow* (and yes, I realise I'm showing my age by referencing *Willow* rather than one of the *Harry Potter* films)! This was huge, and certainly worth massive bragging rights if you were a teenager in the mid-nineties.

I was slightly apprehensive the first time Stuart, my twin brother James, and I went to the cinema by ourselves because just as we were getting out of the car, Stuart's mum turned to James and I and handed one of us a small box. She then proceeded to tell us that it contained Stuart's emergency epilepsy medication—in suppository form. Getting blank looks from the two of us, Josie then explained what we'd need to do, and where we'd need to put it, if Stuart had a fit. We must have looked like two startled deer in a car's headlights.

But the memory I keep coming back to is one of my newest. I was recently back home for my little sister's wedding, and while I was back, I got to spend a lot of time catching up with Stuart. He was confined to a wheelchair after surgery to repair broken bones in his feet. But despite being in plaster and having screws in his feet, he was still his usual happy, positive, and joking self.

Knowing Stuart for as long as I have, the impact of his disabilities has lessened over time to the point now where I don't even notice them, partly because they are now somewhat normal to me, but mostly because Stuart has learned to live with them, adapt to them, and not let his disabilities define him. But this time, things were different—for me anyway. There was a whole new set of limitations for me to get my head around; finding the nearest drop curb before we crossed the street, making sure the restaurants we went to had good disabled access, that sort of stuff. Stuart, in typical fashion, took all of this in stride; it was me who had to adjust my thinking.

I think that's the point I want to end on and hope what you will take from this book in general. Disability is not something that has to define a person. It's something that can be accepted and blended into one's life through the strength and resolve of the person living with the disability, but also through the actions of others and their willingness to approach new situations with an open mind and an open heart.

Love you, brother.
B.

ACKNOWLEDGEMENTS

This book has been a big undertaking for me, but it would not have been possible without the help, support, input, and encouragement from some very special people.

I am very thankful to my mum and sister, Simone, for helping me remember everything that has happened.

I will be eternally grateful to John and Nicki Broughton for being my first editors and whipping this book into shape. Thank you for all your support and encouragement. This book would not have been possible without your help.

Thank you to my lifelong friends Bradley and James Fairbrass for writing the forewords to this book. I am blessed to have you in my life. You will always be my brothers.

Thank you to my Uncle 'Billy' Charles Swift who guided me towards self-publishing.

Thank you to James Boughton of Commonlight for doing such a fantastic job with the photographs on the cover.

When I needed input and encouragement, Rachel Ward, Adam McGeever, Sandi and Jason Frost, Dani and Dave Alderson, and Clare Durling gave me it. Thank you from the bottom of my heart.

Thank you to everyone at AuthorHouse, who made the publishing process as enjoyable as possible.

Thank you to the rest of you who have encouraged me during this project. Your kind words kept me going.

INTRODUCTION

I was dead for twenty-six minutes. That is how my life started. It sounds like a film that begins at the end. All that ensued was a result of how I arrived in this world.

I don't remember being sat down by my parents, with or without the doctor, and being told I had cerebral palsy. I know that the 'talk' must have been when I was young, because I seemed to have had a grasp on at least the minor details of my disability from an early age. But the actual moment of truth was never etched into my brain by my memory engraver.

Given my lack of recollection of my first discussion about my cerebral palsy, I can quite safely say that it wasn't a life-shattering revelation. Nothing suddenly fell into place or suddenly made sense—nor did I fall to my knees and beat the floor whilst crying upwards, 'Why? Oh why?' Later on, in my teenage years when frustration and isolation set in, I would ask 'Why?' But children are resilient, and in my initial blooming phase I can't say I wasted too much time being upset about the new words that had been pinned to my chest.

I was deprived of oxygen at birth, which led to being a stillborn baby. I was born. I was dead. It sounds like an oxymoron. For twenty-six minutes the doctors tried to resuscitate me. They were just about to stop trying when I took my first breath. It will be no surprise to you when I say that the number twenty-six holds great significance for me. I have the number twenty-six in Roman numerals tattooed on my right arm. Every tattoo I have represents something in my life, but my twenty-six tattoo has a special meaning attached to it because that is where my life started.

If I hadn't started breathing in the twenty-sixth minute, I wouldn't be writing this book.

Being dead for twenty-six minutes is one reason for the title of this book. The other reason has a bit of fate imbedded into it, if you believe in such things. I embarked on the journey of writing this book when I was twenty-six years old. When coupling these two reasons, it seemed to make sense that I simply call the book *26*.

My disability is imprinted on my soul. As an adult, I know that the cerebral palsy shapes me rather than defines me. Cerebral palsy and I are like two trees that somehow became tangled, and we have had to grow together. When I was younger however, I did not have such understanding. I felt that the cerebral palsy allowed me no quarter, and so I gave it none with my scathing opinion of the condition. I was a 'cerebral palsy person' rather than a 'person who has cerebral palsy'.

I tried to hide my disability because I thought it made me look ugly, which, looking back, conjures up an image of attempting to hide an elephant in my back pocket. This was especially the case with people who I was meeting for the first time. I believed they would only see my disability, but in actuality that may have been all I saw at that point in my life.

It takes time to come to an understanding with one's disability, and then, when you think you have struck an accord, your condition—or as I nicknamed it, my body's housemate—decides that confrontation is so much better than cohabitation.

There is no magic wand when it comes to reconciling yourself with any disability; however, after the shackles of conformity are thrown off when one leaves school, it becomes easier to find one's own way. There is a lot of pressure to fit in at school. It can seem as if you are swimming against a strong current if you feel you don't fit in. But when school is finished, you can find yourself in a lagoon where there are fewer currents, and you can choose which way to go.

Of course, it is not as simple as that, and I have had knocks that have tested my resolve throughout my life. I have tripped up and have had to get back to my feet. Every now and again I will be tested by an obstacle that will lead me to doubt my ability to cope and overcome the situation. As a child, obstacles that would test my resolve were simple things like not being able to ride a two-wheeled bike. By the time I was a teenager, I worried that my disability would scare away girls who might otherwise have been interested. Adulthood rolled around, and I wished I was still worried about riding a bike. Now, I find myself worrying about whether my disability will affect my ability to do a particular job or a simple household task.

Dealing with disability can be like riding a bull. As you ride the bull, it bucks one way and then the other, trying to throw you off. If the rider fights the bull, the rider is more likely to be thrown from the animal's back and hit the floor with a thud. But if riders accept that the bull is going to try to throw them off, and they simply go with the flow, then the so-called 'most dangerous eight seconds in sports' become eight seconds of freedom, and they are more likely to stay mounted. My twenties, for the most part, have been about trying not to fight my cerebral palsy symptoms.

An example of this would be eating food. My hands can shake or, to use the bull reference, buck, because of my cerebral palsy. I have tried to control these involuntary moments, but that is like trying to control the bull. My hands become two separate entities, and they seem to be in control of the rest of me rather than the other way around.

When my hands start to shake whilst I am eating, I now try to breathe deeply, relax, and realise it just may be one of those days when my hands decide that they want to impersonate an earthquake. The trick is accepting that to have one of those days is okay, and it doesn't make me less of a functioning person. In truth, it actually makes me a higher-functioning human being, as I am able to adapt to the situation and succeed in eating my food.

Years pass by and experience stacks up. The food experience may sound cringe-worthy, but it is an example of how my disability trickles through every crack and cranny of my life. For this reason, I didn't want to merely write a book about my disability but rather how it infuses my life, bringing different adventures to the fore. The very essence of this is being held in your hands at the moment. I am 100 per cent sure that I would not be writing a book about my life if I wasn't disabled.

In the early nineties, an Australian comedian called Steady Eddy came to my family's attention. This particular comedian appealed to us because he had cerebral palsy, and he was using his condition as material for his act. I wouldn't say the penny I was holding dropped, but my grip was loosened slightly, and I saw that there just might have been a bit of method to my parent's madness that was akin to Steady Eddy's routine. My parents always encouraged a siege mentality based on humour to get me through the trials that life with a disability threw at me.

My father, like my own personal Nostradamus, gave me a glimpse into the future when he described a scene that would be reoccurring in my adult social life. Dad told me that one night I would be in a pub, and my unsteady balance and shaking hand would contrive to spill my drink on someone, or I would fall into the person, spilling his or her drink everywhere. Dad said that in those situations and others, I would need to be able to fight or—the safer option—be able to defuse the situation with a joke, quip, or comment. I can still remember the example he gave me. Believe me, if it were on a CD or DVD it would be worn out by now due to the amount of plays it has had. 'I'd like to see how well you would carry a drink after you'd been dead for twenty-six minutes!' The 'put-down' is as adaptable as an egg and can be applied to many situations, such as, 'I look good for being dead for twenty-six minutes!'

Some people may call this tactic self-deprecation, but I think that is a little too cut and dried. There is some self-protection at work in that I am disabling the attack. I have taken the ladder from underneath that person, and he or she now has nowhere to go. If anything, I find this tactic more self-appreciating than self-depreciating. When sound bites of that particular nature are required, I just go into automatic response, but when I write them down, they come across to me as big compliments: I do look good for being dead for so long, and it is not an easy task carrying a drink when you have cerebral palsy. What some people may call a protection mechanism, or making fun of myself, can be the best example of the old adage that much truth is spoken in jest. If you are somewhat sceptical or disagree with me at this stage, I hope you will understand my point of view by the end of the book.

For most of my life, I have strived to be part of the establishment, to be seen as normal, to be accepted, and to be popular. But as I got older, I started to embrace alternative points of view. I started to listen to alternative music, and I developed empathy for the antiheroes in popular culture who didn't care if they fitted in. I reduced the amount of slang I used and widened my vocabulary. I still wanted to be popular, but I no longer wanted to conform. This book has been a journey—visiting places that I could never forget and remembering things that had slipped into the doldrums of my mind. It is a story about the first twenty-six years of my life: the experiences I have had and the people I have met along the way that have been part of this evolution of self.

1

Who Wants to Be a Millionaire?
I Do!

Valentine's Day 2005 was my red-letter day. I felt like Julius Caesar when he led his troops to the banks of the Rubicon and realised there was no going back. Things would never be the same. On this particular day, I agreed to a financial package to settle my court case against the National Health Service (NHS) for a sum of one million pounds. I had sued them for negligent care during my birth, asserting that their substandard care was the reason I had sustained brain damage and thus cerebral palsy.

There are times you feel that your life will change forever—when you leave school or university or when you find someone who is really special. Sometimes those days are exactly that—life changing. However, I have often found such fleeting moments to be false dawns. The pivotal moment that is in front of you, masquerading as a most tangible object, transforms into vapour, and you realise that nothing has changed. For my family and me though, Valentine's Day 2005 was not an imposter looking for a quick getaway. It was the new dawn we all had hoped for.

London is a city steeped in culture, but it didn't mean anything to me. I wasn't part of London's history, but on this day, it became part of mine. Mum and I glanced at the steps of the Old Bailey. We were scheduled to walk up them and into a courtroom in one week's time, but now it appeared unlikely that we would. They had looked so daunting on previous visits; there were so many steps. It seemed as if you would experience altitude sickness if you made it to the top. Now they looked like steps to a bungalow, unnecessary steps that hopefully we would never have to climb. I felt the exuberance of a child as I hummed the nursery rhyme 'Oranges and Lemons': 'When will you pay me? say the bells of Old Bailey.' As it turned out, pretty soon!

Mum and I walked towards the law court offices. I was not wearing a coat, so the wind seemed to go right through me and back again. It was whipping up all the nervous energy inside me like a pile of leaves whirled into a mad frenzy. After the meeting with my legal team, Mum and I walked out of the building—and I was carrying my new surreal status of being a millionaire. The wind had a different feel about it; it now felt refreshing and crisp. When we walked, it was helping us along, as if we were being given a boost. Our spirits were high, and we rode the wind right up to cloud nine. We kept our heads firmly in the clouds for the whole trip home and for a couple of weeks after that.

We had started our journey with the court case in 2000. During that time, the case had taken up a large amount of my family's life, especially my mum's and mine. We walked around with heavy weights on our shoulders, just waiting for someone to surgically remove them. We had to jump through hoops as we went through countless interviews, meetings, and assessments. We had been through a string of different solicitors and two law firms over the course of the five years, and we had seen the court case go from being strong to being on the brink of collapse; the case was more unpredictable than the British weather! We had gone through a lot of heartache to get to this point.

Life in the twenty-first century is driven by the ease of communication. As we walked back to the tube station, I began texting and ringing my friends to tell them my news. I rang my best friend Adam McGeever to tell him 'it' was settled. I texted another friend, Nick, who rang me whilst I was on a train winging my way back home to Peterborough. It was such a surreal conversation. After the 'well done', et cetera, et cetera, our conversation went like this:

> Nick: 'Did you get any Valentine cards?'
> Me: 'No, just a million pounds from the NHS!'
> (At this point most of the other passengers started looking at me.)
> Nick: 'You can't really beat that.'
> Me: 'No, you can't!'
> Mum: 'I think you better hang up now.'
> Me: 'Nick, I'm going to have to go now; everyone is staring at me!'

As I bathed in wave after wave of excitement about the conclusion of the case, I was presented with a problem. I was just shy of twenty-three years old. I know how it sounds: 'A problem? A millionaire by the age of twenty-three? Is he having a laugh?' And I agree. I did have everything. I had financial security, I bought my dream house, and within two weeks I fell in love for the first time. I had obtained in one month what most people would strive their whole lives to achieve. But where does one go from there? I had fulfilled all of my ambitions by twenty-three. I wasn't greedy; all I wanted was money, a car, a house, a pool table, and sex—not necessarily in that order. Now I didn't have any motivation to help me focus on something. I must say though that I wasn't bothered. I left my job and decided to live the life of a young millionaire who was in love. I do not regret it for a minute; I owed it to myself, and everyone who helped get me there, to take it easy.

I didn't really know where to go from that point. My whole life had been shaped by a fight of some kind related to my disability. I had always had challenges to grapple with, be it struggling with my health, trying to pass exams, or fighting a court case. Suddenly the court case had been settled, and I had no apparent fights left to fight. In those golden two weeks after the conclusion of the case, I had bought my dream house and met a girl. Perhaps drunk on euphoria and momentum, I felt love for the first time. Bliss would be a good word to describe what I was experiencing. For the first time I was not dictated to by my disability; I was in charge of the cerebral palsy rather than the other way around.

I could have found a new challenge in working for my new boss at the cleaning company where I was the assistant manager. Mum had owned the business but had sold it after the court case finished. The new owner was not easy to deal with, but I just could not muster enough motivation to rise to the challenge. He just seemed to be the personification of a small fish compared to foes I had faced in the past. In my head, I was a dragon slayer. My sword still had NHS blood on it, and so when I heard that my next *tête-à-tête* was to be against Mickey Mouse, I did not feel the same blood lust that I had felt before. I was the one in charge of my cerebral palsy, and I applied that feeling to my professional life and decided to walk away.

In the film *Scarface*, the lead character Tony Montana looks up at the sky and sees a blimp that says 'The world is yours.' I felt as if I'd seen this airship in my life's sky; I thought I had it all: love, my new house, and my financial settlement. Maybe if the girl I had been involved with had been different, it might have worked, but it turned out that my newfound life outlook put a strain on our relationship. The girl had not been around for the previous five years whilst the court case was going on and never grasped the true nature of what my family and I had been through—nor what we had achieved. The girl thought I was doing nothing with my life, but I was enjoying doing nothing. Unfortunately, she became the fight that my life had been lacking, and bliss was pierced on a regular basis.

She was the first challenge in my life that was counterproductive for me. In February 2005, I stood on a beautiful shoreline that had withstood the strongest seas, but as time went by, the waves crashed on the shore and started to erode the rocks that had seemed impenetrable only a short time before. As the sea continued its relentless assault on the strong shoreline, the resolve and appearance became less impressive, and the shoreline started to crumble. That was my confidence in the relationship. I was no longer free. Not only had my disability shackled me, but my relationship had as well. It came to pass that I had two masters—the cerebral palsy and the girlfriend.

Please do not think I am trying to say, 'Poor me, poor me, I have a million pounds'. I felt great that the court case was over. I had been in life's waiting room for five years while the legal battle went on, and there had been a feeling that when it was all over I could get on with my life. Unfortunately, it wasn't as simple as that. I should have been catching my breath and taking a bit of time to find out things about myself that I didn't know. I should have just gone on a long holiday and let everything sink in. Alas, I didn't do that. I made lots of decisions that were a mixed bag of good and bad.

There are different kinds of fighters. I am not a physical fighter, but throughout my life I have had to fight to overcome challenges that my disability had thrown into my path. I had a 'What now?' syndrome after the court case, because I had never really been able to put the cerebral palsy and all that comes with it on pause. I was finally able to do that on Valentine's Day 2005, and that is why starting this book with that day seemed to be appropriate. However, even the days that change your life cannot keep it on pause forever. Valentine's Day 2005 was like a chapter ending my first twenty-two years because it concluded the fight with the NHS and it righted the wrongs of my birth—but in life there are always more chapters.

2

I Am the Resurrection

If something is hard to deal with or comprehend, at times, I have leant on humour in order to keep me upright and allow me to face what makes my head spin. In my teenage years, the easiest way for me to keep my anger at bay when talking about my birth was to wrap myself in a blanket of blasphemy. I used to say that Jesus and I were one and the same because we were both resurrected after death. This statement always evoked some kind of reaction, be it laughter, anger, intrigue, or in some isolated instances, agreement. It was a way of turning the anger I felt outwards and kicking it as far away from me as possible. If I had been making two piles when I was growing up—one To Deal with Now and the other To Deal with Later—my birth would have been put firmly at the bottom of the later pile.

I would reason with myself that I was telling the story of my birth with humour and adding the Jesus line to make it less harrowing for the listener, but in truth, it was also to make the tale less harrowing for me. I would have a sense of gratification if I made people laugh when telling them about my birth, and consequently, my anger would be numbed.

I stand before you now, well, figuratively at least, to tell you the story about my birth—without trying to use humour to mask my anguish or to make you laugh.

Mum and Dad met in early 1979. After two weeks, Dad proposed to Mum, and in November they were married. Similar to being on the Waltzer's at the fair when the carny adds a little more velocity with a less-than-gentle push, my sister arrived in 1980. I transformed the whole family funfair into a white-knuckle, roller-coaster ride when I arrived in 1982.

My mum's second pregnancy was smooth sailing. After having Simone, she was told that she should never have a normal birth again due to her small pelvis. Acting on that advice, Mum and Dad made their way to the hospital to get an appointment for Mum to have a C-section. The registrar who saw Mum altered my life before I'd even been born. She said that because Mum had given birth naturally before, she could quite easily do it again. "See you when you've gone into labour," she said. This woman opened Pandora's box, and just like when you release a sound in space, it carried on, vibrating through my life for evermore.

I was born on April, 10, 1982. The labour was going fine, and as much as you can, apparently Mum was enjoying the process. After a while, the nurse told Mum the machine monitoring me had stopped working. We now know, in fact, I had stopped breathing. What ensued could only be described as chaos. The nurse went to get the doctor, and the doctor didn't come on time. By the time he arrived, it was too late to do an emergency C-section. The wheels came loose, and Dad was bundled out the door. The doctor forced his hand inside of Mum to try to pull me out. This was a poor decision, because I had the cord wrapped round my neck two times, and I had pulled the placenta away. The doctor was effectively throttling me. The doctors finally got me out using forceps. For just under an hour, these attempts continued, and during that time I had not been receiving the necessary amount of oxygen, which led to me being stillborn.

Mum describes my appearance as grey and bruised. I was rushed away from Mum in order for the medical staff to try to revive me. As I have told you already, I was dead for twenty-six minutes; it was only because Peterborough District Hospital was a teaching hospital that they didn't stop earlier. They were just about to give up when I took my first breath. This close call seems both real and unreal to me. On one hand, it is real to me because I have felt the reverberations for my whole life—it is my inescapable reality. On the other hand, it feels so unreal because it is something that you see on a television programme like *ER*, not something that happens in real life.

My whole life boiled down to a lesson for medical students; if they hadn't been in training, they wouldn't have carried on trying to revive me. It is almost as if my little body got up late and had to run for the bus. Just as the bus was starting to pull away my body jumped on to the bus and said, 'Hold on, I'm here!' As I wrote that analogy, I see that I referred to myself as 'my body' rather than 'me' or 'I', which shows me that I have a kind of surreal detachment surrounding my birth. I know it happened to me, but because I don't remember it, I feel as if I am looking in on the memory rather than being part of the memory.

I think of my birth in a kind of out-of-body-experience way, but for Mum, the night was very real. Fear swelled every minute into an hour. I have visions of everything moving fast but lasting an age. Mum has vivid memories of that night. Her body felt the pain of that night for years afterwards. She can remember the snapping noise when I was brought out of her. She remembers the grey colour of death that dominated my body. She remembers the doctors rushing me away from her so that they could keep me alive. Her heart was beating so fast that she felt it might split her chest open and escape. She watched her worst nightmare unfold in front of her with a sense of pure terror. Something like that stays with you forever. The thought of Mum going through such pain makes me feel as if my insides have been tied to a heavy weight and have been thrown off a cliff. I feel as if I am falling but will never reach the bottom.

Meanwhile, Dad was in limbo in the corridor, not knowing a thing. Dad was not a man who was at ease expressing what turmoil was at work inside of him. He never told me what he went through on that evening when the nurses removed him from the equation before the chaos started. I feel sadness, because I don't know whether he was terrorised by the sounds of his wife in pain or whether he was so scared that he went outside. As a person, I have a thirst for knowledge, but I feel a dull ache inside because I will never know what he went through alone in the hospital corridor. Sometimes I wish I could revisit a time in my life or talk to somebody I love who is no longer with me. I really wish I could go back to the night I was born and put an arm around my dad in that corridor and talk to him.

Dad may have been in denial or complete shock, because when Mum told him the whole story afterwards he thought she was exaggerating events. Maybe Dad and I were a lot alike in that hearing about my birth was not enough to allow us to comprehend what happened or the extent of what we heard. Dad may have been angry like I was, and that would have made understanding what Mum was telling him impossible. I could suggest reasons all day, but the ones I have written down seem to make the most sense to me.

I was whisked off to the special care unit where I continuously fitted throughout the night. Mum endured a night of dread as she lay awake on the ward. She thought that every set of footsteps she heard belonged to a doctor who was coming to tell her that I had died. She was alone with her thoughts. Dad was with my sister, and he had not yet been fully read in on the horror that Mum had been subjected to. Exhaustion, emotion, pain, and worry conjured up thoughts of tragedy in Mum's head. An anxious fire burned in her stomach and the smoke swirled around her head, filling her mind with every scenario she could imagine. Mum was not paranoid. Her imagined scenarios were very real, which meant that Mum could not discount any of them. Nights like that are elastic, and they stretch on and on until time doesn't have authority any more. The only mark in the sand that Mum's mind didn't kick over was waiting for daylight and the chance to ask a doctor or nurse whether I was still alive.

I didn't die that night; something in me decided that it was too early to check out of the hotel, and so I battled on. My first night on this earth set the tone for the rest of my life. It was akin to being at a concert where the band has played its first song in a way that is awe-inspiring. The hair on the back of everyone's neck is standing up. The band members look at each other and say, 'We've got to keep this going', and the people in the crowd look at each other and say, 'This is going to be one hell of a concert!' I may have been late arriving on the stage, but I wasn't going to be pushed off so easily.

After surviving the first night, I spent a week on the special care unit. The nurses loved having me in the unit because I was such a big baby. I weighed eight pounds ten ounces.

The nurses were so used to looking after babies who had been born premature that to be able to handle me as you would a normal baby was a novelty.

At the end of a hurricane, when all the weather calms down, the people come out from their houses to see what damage the storm has caused. I stopped fitting after a few days, and as my parents looked on, it appeared that my particular hurricane had blown through me, letting me escape with only having the hinges knocked off one side of my body. I was paralysed from my neck downwards on my left side. Still, hinges are repaired after hurricanes, and even if they squeak or creak a bit from then on, at least they still work. The early signs suggested that I had been lucky, and I was allowed to go home, but my family did not realise that the storm had not gone away.

If Dad was in denial, disbelief, or shock when it came to Mum's account of my birth, the first night reached out and slapped him out of that daze, and my problems became just as real for him as they were for Mum. Peterborough District Hospital had packed us up and sent us on our way with medicine in hand. Unfortunately, the hospital had not finished adding to their collection of blunders concerning my care. They gave my parents a different medication than what I had been taking during my stay in the hospital. I was given banana-flavoured medicine when I was in Intensive Care, but the hospital sent us home with strawberry medicine clutched in our hands. When Dad gave me my magic potion, I stopped breathing. Dad had been a fireman when he was younger, which meant that his training kicked in straight away, and he acted on pure instinct. He saved my life. Not many people can say they cheated death twice in their first week on this earth. My family must have felt like a speed bag that boxers use to train—every time they bounced back from an incident, another punch would send them flying.

My parents phoned the hospital to see whether they should bring me back in. The hospital told them to keep an eye on me and to ring again in the morning. After what seemed like two false starts in an athletic race we were off and running. Everyone had their fingers crossed that all of our problems were behind us. But that hope was to be dashed.

My parents benefitted from me being a second child as they started to notice that things with me were not as they should be. I had a slight case of Bell's palsy on the left side of my mouth. This is a form of facial paralysis that stems from facial nerves not working properly. The result is an inability to control the facial muscles on the affected side. My parents had to massage my left arm constantly as I had a case of Erb's palsy. This particular palsy is caused by an injury to the nerves surrounding the shoulder, and the symptoms are a weakness or paralysis in the arm. As the days went on, my arm still hung by my side like a pirate at the end of a noose. Over time, my parents would try to get me to sit, but that also aroused suspicions because my posture was stiff and unnatural, which made my parents worry.

At my godparent's house one Sunday afternoon, I raised hopes—only to dash them again. After not crawling at all, I rose to my feet unaided and walked across the room. After seventeen months of seeing me immobile, everyone was relieved, but it was not to last. I didn't walk again until I was two. Alarms bells were ringing for my parents. I did not sleep through the night for the first eighteen months of my life. I would wake up crying, which must have led my parents to feel bewildered and frustrated. There did not seem to be an end to my cries, and my mum and dad did not know where to turn.

Getting the doctors to listen was a constant challenge for my parents. Mum told a health visitor who came to see her that she was struggling to cope with me crying all the time; the health visitor replied, 'Well, if you give in, he's won!'

Undeterred, my mum and dad pursued the NHS. The first stab at a diagnosis that the doctors provided was that one leg was shorter than the other. This boggles the mind, trying to explain how all my symptoms could be explained away by the odd centimetre or inch being out of sync. Sometimes doctors' diagnoses felt like the attitude that Britain had about the First World War; 'We'll make it a quick campaign, and we'll be home before you know it!' I think it must have been easy to either accept this diagnosis or just give up, but my parents were unsatisfied by this poor explanation and they got back into their tanks and continued knocking walls and doors down in search of answers.

Frustration reached boiling point for my dad, especially when a doctor proclaimed that the only thing wrong with me was that I was a 'clumsy child'. Dad had more than a slight inkling to convey his opposition to this 'diagnosis' with his fists, but instead my parents vowed never to see the doctor again. I remember when I was in my early teens, Mum, Dad, and I went to see a new consultant for the first time. We didn't even have a name, and when the doctor came to call my name it was the doctor who thought I was just clumsy. Mum leant back aghast and said, 'We're not seeing you!' But the doctor said, 'A lot of water has gone under the bridge, come on.' I am sure I saw some traces of egg on his face though.

After eighteen months, we finally had the blindfolds loosened and taken off. My parents were told that I had cerebral palsy. People who have not endured such bewilderment and confusion over why their child is the way it is may find it strange, but my parents felt waves of relief flow over them. They finally had an answer to the mystery, and they could go away and unravel it all by finding the answers to their questions. There was no Internet at that time, but Mum and Dad bought every book about cerebral palsy that they could find. After the struggle for a diagnosis, my parents were standing on a cliff looking down at water below. There were rocks in the water and many unknown quantities, but they had to take the jump into the world of cerebral palsy.

A Report: the definition and classification of cerebral palsy April 2006 is the source that the charity, Scope uses to describe what cerebral palsy is:

'A group of permanent disorders of the development of movement and posture, causing activity limitations that are attributed to non-progressive disturbances that occurred in the developing fetal or infant brain . . .'

My parents may have read something similar, or they may have read something vague describing cerebral palsy as an *umbrella term* covering a group of symptoms and a lot of jargon about the *cortex* as well as the *cerebrum*. These terms can sound overwhelmingly vague, especially since there are countless degrees of severity that come with cerebral palsy.

A person with cerebral palsy may experience involuntary movements or spasms. A person may have speech problems that vary from a slight impediment to being unable to speak at all. The person may have abnormal muscle structure or stiffening of their joints. The person may have problems with sight or hearing, or they may have a mental deficit. These are just a few of the 'could have' or 'may haves' that my parents were facing. Reading about cerebral palsy exposed them to an avalanche of symptoms, and the scary thing was that they did not know how mild or severe my condition was going to be.

The 1980s did not provide a vast array of options that would improve my cerebral palsy. One risky operation included a procedure for stretching the tendons in the back of my heel in order to encourage normal leg growth. At the time, an operation of that sort involved a lot of pain and significant risk factors. If I had had the operation, my legs would have been in plaster and inactive for a long time, which my parents thought would have a detrimental effect on my development. They were unwilling to take a chance on a procedure that might not even work. My parents relied on physiotherapy and exercise to improve my body. Nowadays there are different types of treatment open to children who have cerebral palsy, such as medication, braces, and surgical procedures to repair dislocated hips or curved spines.

My parents were dealing with these decisions blind because it was not until I got older that the main features of my disability came to the fore. As it turned out, my main cerebral palsy symptoms are thus: I have fine-motor-skill issues because both of my hands and arms shake. Sometimes I have good days, when my arms look like tree branches being blown by a gentle wind; on other days my arms can shake a lot like a tree experiencing a strong wind. I have a slight speech impediment: when I speak, I slur some of my words, and sometimes my mouth looks as if it is struggling to get the words out. Again, my speech has good days and bad days. Those who know me well are tuned into my speech frequency. If you spend a little time around me, it is not hard to gain an ear for my 'Stu Slur', but on rare occasions, people who I have just met can have difficulty understanding me. I drag my right foot slightly when I walk. It is not noticeable enough that I would be picked out in the crowd straight away, but a trained observer might spot me. If I ever hurt my left foot, it provides a dilemma, because how can I limp with my left when I already limp with my right?

My left side recovered from the Erb's palsy I suffered from when I was born, but I still have a weakness in those limbs. I have a muscular physique, but if you compare the muscles on my left to those on my right, you will see that the ones on my left are ever so slightly smaller.

I find it hard to say whether I have severe or mild cerebral palsy, because the condition does make its presence felt in most if not all of my life. But at the same time, many of my brethren have symptoms that are much worse than mine. Cerebral palsy does not just affect how they live their lives; it stops them from living their lives how they want to. People get embarrassed and chastise themselves around me by saying, 'Oh, I shouldn't be complaining considering all the things you've had to deal with!' To which I reply that everyone has experiences that are individual to him or her which are not diminished when they are compared to someone else's. And in a way, this applies to disability as well: a disability affects one person in a different way than it does another, hence it is as severe to your life as you feel, and it cannot be compared.

My parents took the drug of knowledge, and after the initial rush of finding out that I had cerebral palsy had faded, the comedown waved its ugly head. It is quite common that when parents find out their child is disabled they will enter a state of grief. They have to grieve for the child that they, in effect, have lost. It's perfectly natural. The child that my parents thought they were going to have was gone, and he took with him all of the hopes and dreams that they had for him. My parents were left with a completely different kettle of fish, me. They seemed to handle it very well: Mum and Dad flung themselves into doing physiotherapy exercises with me, and they worked tirelessly on my speech and my reading skills because they felt that if my body was not going to work properly, they would make damn sure that my brain did.

I was too young to remember this part of my life, but it was very traumatic for us all. The first eighteen months were like the line in the song 'Amazing Grace', 'I was blind but now I see'. My parents were stumbling around the room looking for the light, and although when they found the switch they were confronted with a whole new set of problems, at least they could face them in full sight.

I can't even imagine life without cerebral palsy; I sit looking at the rain falling outside trying to conjure up an idea of what it would be like but I can't. My cerebral palsy is not curable, and it feels as much a part of my body as my heart. I have often wished it was as necessary to me as an appendix, which could be removed, but that is just a case of wishing for something that will never happen. My cerebral palsy has gotten better over time; people ask me if this improvement is common with cerebral palsy, and I have to say I'm not sure. In my case, we never hung around waiting for some magical medicine to save me. My family and I just worked hard to get me to be the best I could be, and we reaped the benefits. Nowadays there are more methods to help manage cerebral palsy, but I think work ethic and a determination to achieve a higher quality of life still have to be at the forefront for any person who has a condition such as mine. My body flourished like a crop that a farmer has worked hard to grow. I put in the hours with my family, and we were able to enjoy the fruits of our labour.

I was told that if the doctors had delivered me eleven minutes sooner, in all probability I would have nothing wrong with me. That was hard to hear. My life could have had an eleven-minute extreme makeover. I would look in the mirror and not know myself. My life could have been much different if the doctors had been quicker. That is as close to looking into another life as I can get. Looking through the eleven-minute window made me feel sad, but I shut it and closed the curtains when I realised that if the doctors had been eleven minutes slower, I would be dead. Each life has defining moments, it just so happened that my most defining moment was my first.

3

DISABLED APPEARANCE

Our minds are like dartboards. When we are born, we have a brand-new dartboard with no holes or blemishes. As the dartboard gets older, many darts are thrown at it. The holes and blemishes that the darts leave represent worries and insecurities that we collect in our minds as we get older. Most people have at least one thing they are insecure about—something small, such as thinking their feet look weird, or something big, such as thinking they are not as intelligent as they would like to be.

My dartboard stayed in pristine condition for quite a number of years, which is a great thing. Childhood should be a time when you are blissfully ignorant. I had little sense of the restrictions that my disability would place on me. I was going to be a crack commando; I was going to be a policeman like Eddie Murphy's character in the film *Beverly Hills Cop*; I was going to be the next Ryan Giggs, scoring countless goals for Manchester United. My cerebral palsy was there, but I didn't question its presence—like a child wouldn't ask why a sibling was at the breakfast table.

Somewhere along the way, when I reached eight or nine, my dartboard was put up on the wall, and every now and again someone would throw a dart at it. I am not quite sure what the trigger was for this, but the dartboard had been hung. The darts would only punctuate my happiness for a fleeting moment, but just like the American frontier settlers who in various guises came to disturb the American Indians' way of life, more kept coming. Maybe in my mind I began to realise that my cerebral palsy was a dog lead, and it would not allow me to do certain things. When a teacher asked for volunteers for a sports event and I stood up, he looked at me and said, 'Sit down, Stuart.' I thought he was being mean at the time, but as I think of him standing at the door of my year-five or year-six classroom, I can see he took no pleasure in telling me to sit down; actually, his eyes looked sad, and his shoulders slumped slightly. I felt a fair few darts prick my dartboard that day.

So, why did the teacher tell me to sit down? What did I look like as a child? The simple answer to the second question would be a happy child. I was full of laughter and smiles as I bounded forward on unsteady legs. I moved like someone who was trying out stilts for the first time. My coordination was off, and I could bump into anything in my path. My knees were like childhood sweethearts that were always very close together no matter how hard the parents tried to keep them apart. I knew I was unsteady and walked different to other children, but it was not until I watched home videos of my childhood or looked at pictures years later that I saw how much my knees kissed each other. My dad compared my walk to Douglas Bader. He was a pilot in the Second World War who was famous for having tin legs—he had lost both legs in a crash. I don't think that when I was playing war with my friends that that was the kind of soldier I wanted to be.

For some reason, our voices sound different in our own heads compared to what other people hear. I was given a microphone for my birthday one year, and I decided I wanted to be the next *Radio 1* DJ; I wanted to be just like Simon Mayo. I recorded my own radio show on a hi-fi stereo with a cassette deck. The voice I heard when I played it back confused me. I said, 'I don't sound like that, do I?' My voice was slow and a little slurred. It was so monotone that I thought something was wrong with the microphone or the tape—not my voice. That was a dartboard moment for me. I felt embarrassed that people had to listen to what I deemed a horrible voice. I was glad that I couldn't hear the slur in my speech in my head when I talked to someone, because I thought it grated. I couldn't understand how people could talk to me.

My parents took me to see a speech therapist, but we were dismissed quickly because I spoke very well. Despite this professional endorsement, the speed in which sentences came out of my mouth was slower than average. I was later told by my parents that some people would finish my sentences. I harbour some bad feelings about what I see as a very impatient way of conversing with me, even though I cannot remember anyone ever doing it. My favourite song when I was young was the theme tune to the children's show *Postman Pat*, and when I would sing along to it, the pace of my speech would become evident. As the second line of the song started, I would just be coming to the end of singing the first line. It was as if the song was being sung into a cave, and I was the echo. 'Postman Pat, Postman Pat and his black and white cat!' would be followed a second or two later with my echo, 'Cat!' I was completely ignorant to my backing-vocal singing style until my parents informed me of it years later. I was quite disappointed, but it always remained a favourite song of my parents as they remembered my childhood.

Despite my voice being less than speedy, I was a very chatty child, and even after my DJ dreams had been destroyed and my confidence rocked by hearing my voice, I didn't stop speaking. I benefited from a child's mind: I quickly forgot about my speech and got on talking through life. I was around people of all ages, and I cannot remember many instances when I was not understood, which leads me to the conclusion that although my speech was slow, the sentences were well put together, and I couldn't have been that hard to comprehend.

Fashion in the eighties left a lot to be desired: florescent colours, cycling shorts, and shell suits. And in my case, clumpy, hospital-issue boots that resembled clogs. They were supposed to support my ankles and aid my balance. The boots were visually hideous, and I am sure they didn't help me at all. I stumbled around even more with those huge monstrosities weighing my feet down. And the fastening of the shoes was not accommodating for someone with cerebral palsy. They should have been fitted with Velcro, which would have made doing them up so much easier, but instead, I would have to lace them up every time by threading the shoelaces through a series of hooks and then tying them up. I didn't learn how to do my shoes up until I was eight. My fingers had to jump through hoops and hooks before they ever got to the elephant or rabbit ears bow; my hands were marines on a punishing assault course, and they would fall flat on their face when it came to the final part. With the eighties fashion and my awful boots, I looked like a fashion icon from East Germany!

I have a scar over my right eye. I acquired the wound when I cracked my head on a steel fireplace in my family's living room. The result was quite a big gash, and my parents had to take me to the hospital to be stitched up. The doctors and nurses took one look at my body's landscape that was populated by bumps and bruises as well as a cut in need of attention, and they decided I appeared to be a victim of domestic abuse. I can understand a surface diagnosis such as this, but these doctors had my medical records. All they had to do was read that I had cerebral palsy and everything would have come into focus. Instead of putting on their reading glasses to clear everything up, the hospital staff put my parents through the traumatic experience of being questioned as if they were abusing me.

My parents and quite a few family friends tried to teach me how to ride a two-wheeled bike. Alas, it would be sixteen years before I would learn how to ride a normal bike. Can you imagine a teenager being taught to ride a bike in a public park? If camera phones had been in existence at the time, I would have been an overnight phenomenon on YouTube. All efforts to teach me how to ride a two-wheeler crashed down to the floor, just like I did when I was trying to master the skill you are supposed to 'never forget'. In the end, the hospital issued me a tricycle. It's funny, these days all you get from the NHS is MRSA—back in those days they used to give you bikes.

I didn't care what anyone thought back when I was a child; that tricycle was my pride and joy. It was a bizarre machine, a big tricycle with huge handlebars. Its appearance set it apart from the other children's bikes because it was such a massive contraption. In my mind, I was riding a Harley Davison. I loved my Harley Davison tricycle so much that I think I literally rode it into the ground. I would bomb round with all my friends; we even used to hang on to the back of the tricycle on skateboards and fly downhill. I thought it was very cool. I recommend you do this if you ever come to be in possession of a hospital-issued tricycle. Ignorance is bliss though, because when I went to Centre Parks in my early twenties with my family, we hired bikes, which meant a trip down memory lane for me. My family had to make me ride a tricycle so we all could go on a bike ride. I was a bundle of embarrassment. It's sad that we have to grow up and get inhibitions. I do try and recreate that feeling of being invincible that lived within me as a child, but a sad fact of growing up is that true youthful fearlessness becomes slightly unobtainable—although I'll keep trying.

My dad bought one of the big video cameras when they first came on to the market. He looked as though he worked for the BBC with such a massive machine on his shoulder. Consequently, a lot of Simone's and my childhood was recorded, and these memories sit in a cupboard in my house. I struggle to watch them sometimes, because the screen shows me how unbalanced I was, and I feel awkward watching as I stumble around. I feel unsettled; I listen to my speech and I grimace.

I have improved physically over time; for example, my knees, which seemed destined to get married and to stay together forever, grew apart as the years went by. My legs got stronger, and they became straighter. My knees will always have those early years together, but they have grown up to be independent parts of my body. I am glad they still work well together as individuals for the sake of the rest of my body. If my condition hadn't improved, I probably wouldn't wince when I see early footage of myself. I really wish my stomach didn't feel like a blender when I'm reminded of how I used to look. My early years have a deep connection to where I am now and how far I have come, which should give me a sense of pride, but sometimes I struggle with this concept.

A person once gave me some advice about my reactions to seeing myself on television. She said that when she was learning to salsa dance she would constantly apologise to her partner for making mistakes. Her partner said to her that if she stopped concentrating on the odd thing she did wrong, she would be able to see all the things she was doing well. I am trying to apply this story to my impression of what I looked like then and also now. If I discount the voice, my unbalanced walk, and my touching knees, I see that I was just a normal happy boy.

4

My Lennon and McCartney

The caravan spins at high velocity, and time twists. I've been here before. This is what Muhammad Ali called the 'Half Dream Room', where alligators play trombone and neon lights flash everywhere. This is the realm of the seizure. This is my version of being hit by a haymaker, where nothing makes any sense, and the only thing I can do is hang on and wait for my head to clear.

I hang on to my family. They seem to be walking on a bouncy castle because their heads bob up and down. My body is gripped with panic, and yet my head is groggy. I have no idea where I am, but we are at the centre of the universe. My mum is in front of me, reassuring me. She is trying to make me as comfortable as possible. But out of the corner of my eye, a video camera operated by my dad appears. I try to get away from it. I don't want to be seen fitting. I do not understand why he wants to punish me. I wave my hands at him trying to get him to stop. Mum implores Dad to stop because he is upsetting me, and finally he does.

Here lay two different schools of thought. Mum just wanted to protect me and make sure I was safe, but Dad wanted me to learn from the experience as well. He wanted to show me that I didn't thrash around the floor when I had a fit. I was very insecure about what I looked like during the throes of a seizure. Dad's way of disproving my belief was to film the episode.

On the surface, it appears as if these two parents were on such different pages that they would never work well together. My dad was a man of extremes. He was a man who was capable of great acts of kindness, but at other times, he could be very cruel. Mum could lose her temper, but she was much more balanced than Dad was.

To write a chapter exclusively about Mum was hard. I wrote one, but it did not seem to capture Mum's essence; there was something missing. I spent a long time trying to figure out why it was not coming together, and then I realized that Mum was half of a team. Mum and Dad were a bit like Lennon and McCartney. They both were partners who were great on their own, but when they were put together a spark was ignited and something special happened—be that 'A Hard Day's Night' or raising two children.

Dad did not stay on this earth very long. He died when he was forty-two of a heart attack; I was only seventeen. I'm sure he didn't want to go so early. Life can have such a mean streak, and just as Dad was looking forward to watching his children make their way into the world, he was taken away. But while he was here, Mum and Dad made sweet music together.

Inside, my parents were reeling from events both prior to my birth and afterwards. Dad's father had died two weeks before I was born. The funeral took place a week after my birth; my dad must have felt death all around him, as while he was burying his father, he was uncertain whether I would be alive when he returned. Dad did not know the extent of what I went through at birth—or that I had brain damage—but he knew that I was in very poor health. Mum and Dad also had fifteen-month-old Simone to look after. On top of it all, Dad still had to go to work and provide for us.

On the day that Mum and I left the hospital, a doctor came to speak with her. He told her that it would be best for all concerned if Mum walked out of the hospital and left me behind because I would not live long and she was not up to the challenge. My mum was assured that it was for the best, as she could always have more children. It is horrifying to think that this conversation did not take place in the forties, fifties, or sixties, but in the eighties. I find it somewhat ironic that a doctor, whose chief duty is to preserve life, placed so little value in a baby's life. From day one of my life, doctors' opinions, diagnoses, and actions have been unreliable. Mum and Dad ignored the doctor's advice and took me home.

Even with all that being thrown their way, Mum and Dad made a perfect duet from day one. When one of them took lead vocals, the other one harmonized. Mum took the day shift, looking after both Simone and me while Dad was at work. She would carry out all the motherly duties that came with the territory as well as deal with a sickly child who was paralysed down one side and constantly crying. By the time Dad walked in the door, Mum was exhausted, and Dad took over.

Mum has such gentle memories of my dad lovingly bathing me and rubbing my left arm until it came to life and started to move. Every night, without fail, he would hold me in his arms whilst rubbing my left side. My parents were the personification of a team effort. Mum would nurture me and make sure I made it through the day, and Dad would make sure I made it into the future by working with my body to relieve the pain I was in.

The teamwork was a success. And when the cerebral palsy diagnosis was made, they began to work on my brain. My parent's philosophy was that if my body was going to be less able than my peers, my brain was not going to be. They started to educate me even before I was old enough for school; numbers and words, books and building blocks played predominant roles in my early life. I have never felt mentally inferior due to my disability at any point in my life, and my parents' hard work early on must take a lot of the credit for that.

We were four musketeers facing the world with little cavalry. My dad's sister Clare moved in after I was born because she needed a place to stay, but apart from that, Dad did not have a very close relationship with his family. The majority of Mum's family were as helpful as a Polish phrase book in Brazil with regard to helping with our peculiar and eventful life. My parents had great friends, but they had very little other support, which put a lot of pressure on a young couple.

Sometimes I compare my life at twenty-six to my parents' life, and I marvel at how my mum and dad coped. They had two children—one who was disabled—a marriage, a business to run, and a house to keep. It must have been such a terrific strain, and I can imagine that making time for each other must have been difficult. With a disabled child crying non-stop and not developing physically, any two people would find it hard to spend time together just as a couple.

Our lives were filled with smiles, and the air was populated by laughter. We were approached to feature in a pilot television show for a series that the BBC was making, *Here Comes the Weekend*. The concept of the show was simple: it showcased things to do at the weekend. We went to a theme park called Pleasurewood Hills. I still have the video, and what lit up the day's filming was the ease and happiness that we all shared. I can shut my eyes and see the start of the day: I am bounding along with my Douglas Badar walk, holding both my mum and dad's hands. I flout the obvious limitations of my balance by launching forward and swinging through the air whilst hanging on to my parents. The film depicts a family wrapped up in delight, two caring parents and two children in love with their mum and dad.

One word comes to mind when I think of my mum and dad facing those early years with me. Strength. They were young kids, with no real preparation for such a massive undertaking. They didn't just keep their heads above water—they swam. With the help of friends like Caroline, Bozey, Hayley, and Kim (all great friends who we'll come to later), my parents made our own kind of Arcadian dream. The ancient Greeks believed Arcadia was a paradise reserved for those blessed by the gods, who lived their lives according to their ideal. Our life together was less than perfect, but it was ideal for us because we made it work, and the two people at the centre of our world were Mum and Dad. Our environment was challenging and difficult, but having a disabled child did not condemn everyone in our world to a life of purgatory. Strength comes in many different shapes and sizes.

The type of strength that my parents exhibited was that they were able to blend every element of my disability into our lives so that my condition felt as if it fitted in with everything else. Hospital appointments seemed no different from Mum playing netball on a Sunday, and having cerebral palsy was as run-of-the-mill as waking up in the morning. My cerebral palsy was never ignored. It was a big issue that we had to deal with; the condition made me different, but it didn't mean that I was treated differently. I was expected to adhere to the morals that Mum and Dad taught us, and I knew if I behaved badly, I would be subject to repercussions.

In every possible way I was pushed to function independently. I couldn't grip my knife and fork properly, so I was provided with an adapted set of cutlery. The masterminds behind this drive were my parents. They identified my uncompromising, never-give-in attitude and harnessed it into an energy source. I believe they fed off my determination and that helped maintain their motivation and focus. They each had different ways of doing this.

My mum was firm with me, but she was very nurturing. She would push me to make me the best I could be, but she did it in a subtle way. At secondary school, when I was starting to rely too heavily on my wheelchair to get me from class to class, Mum decided that it would be taken away from me, and I would have to walk around school. This act was firm, but it pushed me into a new independent school environment. I was no longer reliant upon anyone to get me to and from class. I was also at head height with my peers, thus, in a literal and figurative sense, no one was looking down on me when we had a conversation. Mum's actions can now be seen by all every time I stand up. As an eleven-year-old, when I stood, my knees appeared to have magnets in them that were drawing them towards each other. Over time, due to the decision to make me walk more often, my legs got stronger—to such an extent that the magnetic power in my knees has disappeared, and I stand up straight. I walk with a slight limp, but if I hadn't been pushed to stand on my own two feet, I probably would be restricted to a wheelchair. Mum's little decision changed one future into another, more mobile life.

Dad's approach was at times far brasher than Mum's. I used to have to dictate my homework to my parents because of my poor handwriting. Dad had mentioned once or twice that my dictation was not precise enough, because I said 'um' and 'er' between words and sentences. Dad assumed the role of scroll one day, and after I had finished dictating the piece of work, he presented me with a page of writing that was punctuated not just by full stops and commas but 'ums', 'arrhs', and 'errrhhhs'. Dad had written down every sound I had made. I was flushed with anger; he looked so pleased that he had proven his point by being so literal. At the time, I thought he was being an awkward so-and-so, because it meant that the homework had to be redone. His actions seemed very excessive to me because my time had been wasted, and Mum then had the task of saving the work of 'umms' and 'arrhs'. Dad had warned me before, and I had not heeded the warning, hence he took matters into his own hands. He was trying to illustrate how clear and concise I had to be when dictating. I was disappointed by his actions, and I think he thought this would spur me on to improve my dictating technique or to find a better method of doing my homework. In a sense, his lesson led me to doing more of my homework on a computer, which has meant that I have been fairly computer literate from a young age. Dad's lessons sometimes puzzled me. Sometimes it is only when I look back that I see he was trying to motivate me through angering me. The reasons and repercussions of the awkward homework encounter have become clearer after writing about it.

Their difference in approach sometimes led to creative differences between Mum and Dad. They were two different people with the same goal but with different routes leading them towards that goal. Sometimes it felt as if Mum was trying to nurture me in this world while Dad was trying to show me the nature of the world. Dad would let me fall over and hurt myself. I must stress that this was not in a mortal-danger kind of way but in a cuts-and-bruises kind of way. He once took me to work with him. We were cleaning Deep Pan Pizza, and the chef made me a pizza. Upon being presented with the pizza, which was fresh out the oven, Dad watched me pick up a slice and bite into it. The whole kitchen watched as I burnt my mouth and stringy cheese flailed from it. I was very embarrassed, and it highlights the difference between my parents: Mum would not have stood back and watched me burn my own mouth. Dad was happy to teach me a lesson.

Our family is Mum and Dad's masterpiece. The Beatles album *Sgt. Pepper's Lonely Hearts Club Band* was one of the first concept albums. The album was considered risky because it was far from conventional, and the record executives didn't know if people would like the music. But the result was something that was inspiring, fun, and gloriously individual. That is how I see my family. We did fly in the face of convention. Doctors who didn't think I'd live long were dismissed. My parents ignored people who questioned if I would walk. Some people thought I wouldn't even be able to use an oven but we scoffed at suggestions like that. I imagine Lennon and McCartney were much the same when they were told that animal noises do not have a place on a pop album.

It takes courage to take up arms against convention. Conventional wisdom suggests that failure will follow those who buck the trend, but my parents never paid attention to the 'witch doctors of orthodoxy'. If Mum was picking a pet, she would always pick the runt of the litter, and Dad had a mischievous streak in him that compelled him to thumb his nose at the accepted perceptions of society. Raising me appealed to certain character traits and that added to their resolve to make me the best I could be. Obviously the qualities they had were only contributory motivators, but the more inner resources a person can draw upon during trying circumstances, the better equipped they are to deliver a positive outcome.

I have a projectionist in my head who plays my memories. Some days I have him play specific memories, and I watch them unfold on the white screen in my brain. On other days, he picks random memories to play for me. The projectionist has just pulled a particular memory out of his box: the scene is that of a lovely, warm Menorca night.

My holidaying family and I are sitting at an outside table eating a meal at a restaurant. We are in a square of some sort and the light looks orange as it illuminates the stony ground. My parents are telling my sister and me about the challenges that faced them whilst I was young—tales of my birth and other difficulties. The projectionist fast-forwards to a particular sound bite, and Mum turns to me and over the street din says 'Stuart, you are my destiny. You are why I was put on this earth.'

My insides feel warm and pride bubbles within me. I never look at how my parents feel about having a son who is disabled; I merely see life through my eyes. But at that moment I am humble. In other cultures, disabled babies are a curse on a family. I am not looked at by my parents as some kind of judgement that brings about bad luck for the family. My family could quite easily harbour feelings of persecution, but instead they take what many would class as a tragedy and turn me into a gift.

One day when I was watching television with Mum when I was a child, Bob Monkhouse was being interviewed. He was speaking about his son who had cerebral palsy: 'Everything that your child with cerebral palsy achieves means so much more to you.'

I asked Mum if that was true, and she answered, 'Yes, it really does.' Was I putting words in Mum's mouth when I asked this question? I don't think I was. I think that every obstacle I overcame, every achievement that came my way, strengthened my parents' resolve and whispered encouragement in our ears—a motivational speaker assertively proclaiming, 'Look at him do that! Doesn't it make the struggles worth it?' The victories helped us through the hard times which always came our way. We had fits to deal with, battles to fight with various people who said that I wasn't disabled, and my disabled badge being taken away from me.

Mum had to go solo when Dad died; she had to hold it all together. I imagine her balancing everyone on her shoulders. Mum took on Dad's business. She didn't want to, but she felt she owed Dad that much, because he would not have wanted his employees to be out of work and left to claim off his estate. At the same time, she continued with her own job as an office manager at the relationship counselling charity, Relate. On top of all that, she continued to be the glue that kept the remaining three members of our family together.

It was far from easy for Mum. Simone and I pulled in different directions, and a lesser woman would have been torn apart at the seams, but Mum wasn't. Even when the threads were coming loose, she regrouped and pulled us back together. We all handled our grief in different ways, which meant that at times we wanted to act in contrasting ways. When one of us was stuck in a wallowing stage, another may have been in a keeping-busy stage. Being of differing mindsets and going through different emotions did put all three of us in opposing corners at times. In this period of our lives, the woods seemed to have closed in on us, the trees seemed to be on fire, and we couldn't see anything in front of us—but we were always able to put the fires out and come back together. This concept of strength was bred into us by Mum and Dad, and at a time when we could have diluted we remained insoluble.

Mum has made it without Dad. She never wanted to, and I'm sure sometimes she stops and fantasizes about where our lives would have taken us if Dad was still here. But parts of the story end and new ones begin. Our lives are stories that are being written as we speak. Maybe there was a reason for Dad to go; maybe he was here to set us on our way in this life. He was far from an angel—he was a flawed individual in many respects, but he did give us the tools to carry on without him. He taught us perseverance, independence, and respect, among many other things. He taught us how to cope. We lose sight of these lessons every once in a while, as everyone does. I, myself, sometimes lose sight of the principle of our family: no one can make it on his or her own. But as a family we are intrinsically linked and that keeps us close to each other.

We hurt as one, and we are happy as one. Mum thinks that we are unlike most families in how close we are. I think every family relationship is individual, and Mum and Dad built one from the foundation up that worked for us. In our family, we have found that to succeed, love isn't all you need. You need strength, determination, and courage as well. Mum and Dad made sure we got bountiful portions of all those necessary nutrients, and they raised two headstrong, independent, loving, and intelligent adults.

5

THE WALLET PHOTO

I was taught a lesson by my dad when I was very young about people's perceptions of the disabled. It was a powerful lesson about people's reactions.

We were holidaying in our usual spot, Hunstanton, on the coast of Norfolk. I found a passport photo of me in my dad's wallet. It was a school photo—the type your parents buy as part of a package containing photos in several different sizes that they disperse to those in your family who want one. I had a massive cheesy grin on my face in the photo, a cliché of any happy child's school photo. It was a picture that a dad would take pride in carrying in his wallet, but for some reason I objected to him having it.

I feel ashamed that I felt that I should have the photo in my wallet even though I did not have a wallet at the tender age of eight. How vain I was to actually want to carry a picture of myself about my person! It wasn't as if I was going to forget what I looked like when all I needed was a mirror. I remonstrated about this, and then came the lesson.

My dad said that beyond the fact that I was his son and he wanted to carry a photo of me as well as a picture of Simone around with him, he had it in his wallet for another reason. He said that when he was talking to people who had never met me he would describe how his son was dead for twenty-six minutes when he was born and how he had been paralysed down his left side for a while. Dad would tell these people that his son has brain damage and suffers from cerebral palsy due to being deprived of oxygen at birth. He would describe to them how I'd walk with my knees pushed together and how my hands shook.

Dad would then ask his audience, who by this point were drowning in a sea of sympathy, if they would like to see a picture of his disabled son. Dad described the looks on their faces; I like to think of their expressions as an abstract painting full of colours that symbolised a complete range of emotions—fear, embarrassment, curiosity, compassion, sadness, and revulsion. I imagine these people as rabbits peering into the oncoming headlights. They were obviously in a catch-22 situation: if they refused to see the photo, they would look like beings who were devoid of any heart or soul, but at the same time, they didn't want to set eyes on the ugly, disabled creature Dad had described.

Dad would then present the photo, like a poker player who has an ace in the hole, and view the look of surprise and relief on the faces of the captive rabbits. It was as if the car had stopped inches before impacting on the furry bunnies! The photo Dad would show them was of a normal boy, not a drooling mess. I suppose it taught people not to presume that being disabled equates to looking hideous. We are all guilty of preconceptions, and what Dad's story showed me was that one of the tasks that I have, as a disabled person, is to turn those preconceptions upside down.

I have set about doing that ever since, sometimes consciously and at other times subconsciously. I have a drive to prove people wrong, which lives inside of me, but I also set out to do things purely to knock the stuffing out of them. When I was roped into helping a girlfriend's sister move house, I set about proving that the disabled person they had belittled for not being able to do things actually could pull his weight. I made sure I was the one who was the first to lift couches upstairs, and I made sure that I shirked nothing that day. That evening after I had left, they sat about and said, 'We didn't think Stuart would be able to do that!'

My dad's air of mischief allowed him to constantly push boundaries and challenge stereotypes about disability. Dad hired a janitor to work in a department store where he had a cleaning contract. The young man he hired had cerebral palsy. I think that he chose this man rather than the other applicants because he saw a bit of my future in him. After a week, the manager of the store told Dad to sack the janitor because he didn't look right and was damaging the store's image. My dad was a man of principles, and I believe he would have made a stand regardless, but having a disabled son certainly strengthened his resolve and he refused. Again, Dad was bending the barriers of perception with a strong sense of mischief.

By the way, I let Dad keep the photo in his wallet.

6

CIVIL RIGHTS FOR DISABLED
STUDENTS AT PRIMARY SCHOOL

I have a few memories of my first educational experience.
I attended the nursery class at Old Fletton Primary School.
One memory is that I had two girlfriends who I was going
to marry, and they were both named Kim, which seems to
me to be the most ingenious way of making sure that you
never get the names of your two wives wrong. I wonder if
bigamists ever use such tactics. One of those Kims, Kim
Wilmer, has been a big part of my life, as has her sister
Hayley. We grew up together, but Kim and I decided not to
stay together, as we both felt we were too young to settle
down.

The most prominent memory of my time at Fletton Nursery
School is the feeling of detachment I had from the rest
of the class. Much of the time, I was taught on a separate
table away from the rest of the pupils. I was an oddity, and
instead of finding a way to include me in the class, I was

taught in isolation, mainly by the learning support assistant. I think that the school and the staff just did not know how to provide an inclusive education for a disabled child. My parents realised that the school was not going to be able to cater for my needs and this led to them looking for an alternative.

This was the first time I felt I was different to my sister who was in the year above me at the same school. I had no understanding of the different needs that Simone and I would have when it came to our educational environment. I did not feel like my nose had been put out of joint; on some subconscious level I believe I knew that Fletton School was coming up short with my education, and I had to move on. I'm not saying I was able to process what was happening, but it did make sense to me. The only element that made me feel sad was that I would no longer see Simone, Hayley, and Kim, who all went to the same school. Hayley and Kim were as much sisters to me as Simone, thus leaving Fletton made me feel a bit like the odd one out.

My parents had heard about a school in another part of Peterborough that specialised in special-needs education whilst still being a mainstream institution. It was called Matley Primary School. It was different to where I had been going to nursery—rather than keeping me away from the rest of the children, Matley integrated disabled pupils into the class.

I loved Matley! Matley was the polar opposite to my previous school environment. The school was driven by inclusivity; all the students were thrown together, regardless of whether they were disabled or able-bodied. Matley provided a mainstream education for both disabled and able-bodied students, but I think the school gave the pupils much more than that. The school provided a mainstream social experience for the students.

If Matley had purely been a special-needs school, a disabled child's interactions with able-bodied peers may have been limited. And vice versa, if Matley had not enrolled disabled children, able-bodied children may have had limited first-hand experience of being around disabled children. As it was, disabled children learnt how to socialise in a mainstream school environment, which was a microcosm for the real world, and the able-bodied children learnt a greater acceptance of people who were different. To an able-bodied child at Matley, a person who was in a wheelchair was exactly that, a person who was in a wheelchair. To a disabled person there was no fear attached to playing games with the able-bodied student body; a disabled person playing 'Tig' or football with the rest of the boys and girls was commonplace.

Matley's approach to integrating disabled people into the mainstream populations strikes me as being very 'Martin Luther King' in so much as he campaigned for African American civil rights and Matley set about making disabled pupils feel equal to able-bodied pupils. The school was quite revolutionary at the time, because up until then, disabled people had been educated in schools exclusively catering for their needs, which is very much like the segregation that took place in the pre-civil-rights United States.

I met two of my best friends in reception class there: Bradley and James Fairbrass. I would like to give you a recollection of our first meeting but I can't. I can however tell you that when I first went round to their house, we played with their Puff the Magic Dragon toy and then with He-Man! I will talk about these two brothers in greater detail later, but what I will say here is that the Fairbrass family has been one of the most constant parts of my life. We had our childish spats at Matley. I distinctly remember telling Bradley that I hated him just because he was 'going out' with a girl I liked named Emily. The relationship lasted an afternoon, and we were best friends again by lunchtime the next day. The problem with friendships that start on the first day of school is that it is almost impossible to remember the exact reason why we were drawn to each other. One can look for complex explanations as to why things happen the way they do. Maybe I have remained friends with Bradley and James because it just works.

I had my only brush with celebrity dating at Matley. There was a girl named Donna, who was disabled. We were boyfriend and girlfriend in the primary school way of saying we were, but it was more of a ceremonial position that actually had very little responsibility attached to it. We held hands a bit, but that was as far as it went. In truth, our union was more that Donna would say we were going out, and I had little choice in the matter. At the time, there was documentary programme about a children's ward in a hospital, and Donna would often be on the show having treatment. I would say it was quite an achievement to be going out with a TV star before I was even ten.

One thing that was disturbing me as I went through the years at Matley was that the disabled kids seemed to keep dying. It was as if the disabled students were stuffed into one of those toy machines at the amusement arcade, and every once in a while the big silver claw would reach down and pick one of us up and ascend, taking a disabled child upwards and away forever. Every year or so another would disappear, and they would name a bench or a courtyard after them. By the time I was leaving Matley, they were running out of courtyards to name! By now, they are probably naming roof tiles after the dearly departed disabled. My mum and sister tell a story that after one disabled student died I broke down crying, because I thought I would be next. I can't remember that happening, but when the rest of my 'kind' were dropping like flies, it seems perfectly understandable that I'd get a little anxious.

I had two great learning support assistants, and over time, they became an extension of my family. They were Mrs. Dubar and Mrs. Hall. They helped me with my work, looked after me when I had a fit, and made sure that my disability did not hold me back by giving me the tools to work on an even educational playing field. Looking back, it seems that primary school is such an innocent time, no suspicion was levelled against me at Matley for having a helper, but by the time I got to secondary school, having a learning support assistant was like having a bizarre wart on your chin. Pupils would treat me differently and stare at me, and they doubted that I did my own work. At Matley, this was definitely not the case.

In many ways, I wish I could have continued at Matley until I was eighteen. When I was eleven, I had to go to secondary school and leave all my friends behind; they were going to the normal school down the road from Matley. I was going to a school that was more suited to my 'needs'. I hated my parents for making me leave Bradley and James behind. I cried and cried, but they wouldn't change their minds. It worked out for the best in the end, as I got a good education and made some great friends at Jack Hunt Secondary School. I shall never forget Matley—the memories seem to be outlined with gold. I had my problems and sad times at Matley, but the majority of those problems were normal kid's stuff.

I can only speak for my own experiences, but the mainstream social experience that accompanied my Matley education stood me in good stead to go forth into the world and make friends with people whether they were disabled or not. I do not feel I look at my time at Matley through tinted glasses—I did have sad and hard times at the school. There are always going to be exceptions, and not every student embraced the mainstream social experience that Matley offered. The word *spastic* was flung my way from time to time, but there was only so much a school can do. An artist can paint a lovely picture, but it won't be to everyone's taste.

Matley's environment may have been a little too idyllic in a way, because I was not quite prepared for the harsher environment that was waiting outside my primary school bubble. I was comfortable at Matley and a bit more confident; at secondary school it felt like my confidence had been shrunk in the wash. My secondary school was like a sportsman who was compared to the legends that had come before him. It was unfair, but it is human nature to hold two people, teams, or schools up and say which one is better, even if the comparison is not exactly valid. I shall never forget the acceptance that Matley provided. The social and educational experiences will stay with me forever, and I will always be grateful.

7

SPORTS DAYS

It was a bright, sunny day. I was four years old. My mum and dad were in attendance, camera in hand. (You wouldn't get a camera close to a school event these days). I was kitted out in running attire, and I was ready to win the race. I was going to be a blur of blue shorts and a white T-shirt. Everybody was going to fade into the background as I sped away.

I came to the starting line, expectation circulating around my body. The din of proud parents on the sidelines swelled the atmosphere. There were trees that were casting shadows over the finishing line. It was my time! However, I had forgotten that I was disabled and that I ran with the balance of a newly born baby elephant and the speed of a 1970s video game. Or rather, I had not grasped fully the restrictive nature of my disability in certain areas. This was my first sports day and the first competitive environment I had ever been placed in. I was under the impression that when I ran I was faster than the wind, but my lofty opinion of my lightening pace was cut down to size that afternoon.

A hush fell over the crowd. 'Bang!' or 'Whistle!' or even 'On your mark, get set, GO!'—whatever the signal was, the race started. I ran and ran while the crowd of parents whipped themselves into an enthusiastic frenzy. But my vision was not becoming reality. I was at the back of the field chasing dust; it was so embarrassing. I had to check whether I was running backwards and that my lane wasn't made up of quick sand.

The finish line seemed to move farther and farther back. I thought I would never reach the end. My fantasy of winning the race fled the scene and what was left was a victim covered in reality. A worry circled my mind like a solitary vulture: I was concerned that parents would take their children home before I even finished the race.

I did finish, and I was close to tears when my mum pointed out, 'You didn't come in last, Jonathan did!' Unfortunately, it didn't say much, because Jonathan suffered from Down's syndrome, and he had in fact started off the race running the wrong way! Someone had turned him around and sent him on his way. I was so slow that Jonathan nearly beat me.

I was crushed. My virginal taste of failure had been brought forth and forced into my mouth, and it was the flavour of bitter lemons. My parents didn't tell me the reason, but it was slowly dawning on me: I was different. My legs suddenly felt weaker than those of the other children who had beaten me. I didn't look down and see that they looked different as well, but I now had a faint idea that they did not work with the same cohesion as the rest of the pack. My mind of a child—when five minutes feels like an age—leapt into action, and come tea time, I had forgotten my comprehensive defeat.

A different school and a few sports days later, I won the potato-and-spoon race. Sounds like a great triumph over all the odds for a disabled boy, however, it's not as shiny and as much of a Kodak moment as it would first appear. Just before I was about to line up for the practice run on the eve of the sports day, a learning support assistant, who shall remain nameless, instructed me to hold the potato on with my thumb. When I looked at the helper with a certain element of doubt, the instruction was repeated.

Who was I to argue? I am blameless! The potato had even been handpicked for me, because it had a dent the size of a thumb for me to hold. Yes, I cheated! Come race time, I ran with remarkable speed considering I was supposed to have been balancing a potato on a spoon. My feat must have seemed even more remarkable to onlookers when they considered that I couldn't navigate a spoon to my mouth when eating due to my shaking hands, but I was able to sprint all the way to the end without my spoon losing its potato. I felt a tinge of guilt because a girl did tumble over a metre from the end of the race to hand me the win, but I would be lying if I said I felt sorry for how I won. I was like an undercover policeman who had been given permission to break minor laws in order to get the required result. For me, as with undercover police work, the end served the means.

My last sports-day experience was a calamity. The teachers had decided to include the disabled fraternity in the events, and 'we' would be given the task of bringing each race to a close. I loved sports, but for some reason, probably a mix between going out on the high of winning the potato-and-spoon race and anything for a stress-free afternoon, I plumped for this 'easy' job.

I thought the decision seemed flawed at the time, as you really have to question the intelligence of teachers who put disabled children in charge of dropping the bit of string at the finishing line. Unfortunately, this motley crew of disabled students were not known for lightening reflexes and quick hand-to-eye coordination, barring the odd spasm! Consequently, more kids tripped over the finishing line than ran over or through it. We just could not get the hang of dropping the string in time. Our actions really looked like that of a vendetta, 'Take that, you able-bodied show-offs!'

I will cherish the potato-and-spoon victory even though it took place in dubious circumstances. My maiden sports day was the first medium that communicated the affect that my cerebral palsy would have on me. I went from being disappointed, to being elated that I had outwitted the system to win, to being very much on the periphery of proceedings, which to a certain extent is a metaphor for life as a disabled person. Disabled people cannot compete on an able-bodied field all the time, but sometimes, if we can work the system, and hopefully not by cheating, we can gain some advantage back. This may mean that we try harder at school or shine more in an interview situation, but the case can be that if we don't do these things, we can be left on the periphery, watching everyone else run by.

8

WHY HAVE YOU PUT A FLANNEL IN
MY MOUTH?

The issues surrounding my health were complicated in the summer of 1989 when, at the age of seven, a bout of whooping cough triggered a form of epilepsy that I was always likely to contract due to the scarring that had been left on my brain from birth. It was like the deals that you get when you buy a DVD player: buy a Sony Blu-ray DVD player and you get a free film that no one wants to watch!

I felt as if I was taking part in a boxing match and I had been hit by a cheap shot: it hurt and I didn't see it coming. Fits come in different shapes and sizes. My particular brand is a conscious daze where my heads feels as if it has been used as a ball in a baseball game. The first sign that I am about to have a fit is that I get a metallic taste in my mouth, and then the left side of my mouth starts twitching. Not being in charge of my mouth's movement is the most absurd feeling. I imagine a slapstick sketch where I try to stop the twitching by stifling it with my hand, but my mouth swats me away as if I were a fly. I have no say about when the twitching finishes. On some occasions, my mouth has its fun and then decides to stop, but on other occasions, the twitching is just the start of the mayhem.

The twitching may turn to my lips, smacking about like a fish flapping around on deck after a fisherman has caught it. I find it hard to describe what my body looks like when a fit is wringing me out like a flannel because I have always been looking out of my fitting eyes as opposed to looking at my body as an observer. The whole episode is like an invasion, and for the most part, the foreign army swarms down my left side. After the invaders capture my lips, they take my left arm and then my left leg as well, as if the two are held up by high command as being of paramount tactical importance. These limbs feel as though they are attempting to make snow angels, but my right side stands firm and doesn't want anything to do with it.

I can understand how epilepsy has been misunderstood over time. People who have had epilepsy in the past have been seen as being possessed by a demon of some kind. When the fit has run its course, it feels as if I have pushed the demon out of me. The feeling is one of relief, but that only lasts for a moment as my body starts to clean up after the party. The normal post-fit ritual is similar to what happens after a night soaked in alcohol: I would be sick several times, fall asleep shortly afterwards, wake with a thumping headache, and only have the vaguest of memories concerning what happened before I went to sleep.

'The sun was shining, the weather is sweet/Make you want to move your dancing feet.' Bob Marley's words describe a late summer Sunday morning in 1989. The birds were singing, and if you strained your ear, you could hear the washing on the line flapping in the wind. All was quiet as I sat in the living room at home waiting for Dad to say, 'Time to go.' Mum was off playing netball, and Dad was looking after Simone and me. We were getting ready to go out. I was sitting in front of a turned-off television when everything turned hazy; the walls seemed to contort into a fuzz as the fit began.

I didn't know what was happening, but the next thing I knew, Dad had me in his arms and was carrying me out to the car. He put a wet blue flannel in my mouth and told me to bite down on it. I bit down and felt the moisture squeeze. I could feel the texture of the flannel as water seeped out of it. The doctors later told my parents never to put a flannel in my mouth again if I was having a fit, but at the time Dad was falling back on the medical training he had received when he was a fireman.

It is ironic that I had been going to hospitals all my life, but until that Sunday, I had never made it on to a ward. On that ward, my senses took in the environment: the whole place smelt of disinfectant, and the curtains were covered with multicoloured clowns and balloons. I don't know who thought clowns would be a good theme for the curtains, because as far as I am concerned, they are the scariest things at the circus—even scarier than the lions. I wonder if a think tank had been formed and given the brief: 'How can we make the hospital even scarier for children?'

When I lay back on the bed, the sheets were harsh to the touch—an unforgiving landscape that was bumpy, creased, and devoid of any comfort. Lying in that bed was a scary and uncomfortable experience. I was uncertain of what had just happened, and my discomfort was amplified every time the curtains were drawn to surround me with scary clowns armed with balloons. I wasn't impressed by the ward; I just wanted to go home. I cannot remember the doctors examining me. I can only remember my parents telling me what a fit was.

Initially the episode was classed as a one off, and we got back to our normal lives. But when I had another fit, our bubble was firmly burst. The doctors conducted some tests and concluded that I had epilepsy. I had mixed feelings about this new addition. This was not a multipurpose accessory that enhanced my life. Epilepsy was as useful as trousers without any holes for my feet to come out. Despite this, I found being sent off to Addenbrookes Hospital in Cambridge to have an ECG rather exciting. A doctor attached so many wires to my head that I looked as if I had dreadlocks. He then used these wires to see what was going on in my brain. The ECG machine printed out my brainwaves, and the doctors analysed the results for signs of epileptic activity. I thought the whole day was a bit of an adventure: I had been hooked up to a mind reader, and I had been given a printout of my results.

The confirmation that I had epilepsy didn't scare me initially. To me, it was an illness that had ambushed me a few times, but I was under the impression that it would soon crawl back to the hole it came from and let me be. I didn't realise that the epilepsy had been caused by the scarring on my brain that I had incurred at birth and had been laying low, waiting to strike. In a way, epilepsy had been cerebral palsy's sleeping partner, and now it wanted to take a more active role in my life.

The first noticeable change to my body's regime is that I had to take medicine every day. The first medicine we tried made me irritable and tired, and so we tried several others until we struck upon a drug called Tegretol, which came in tablet form. I took the drug twice a day. I felt quite grown up when I started taking tablets because I had only ever had medicine in liquid form.

Mum bought lots of books to help explain to me what epilepsy was. I liked how one particular book used symbolism to describe how a fit starts. It said that it was like throwing a stone into a pond, which causes ripples to flow through the water. In medical terms, it meant that an impulse in my brain sparks off a chain reaction that spreads over my brain and causes a fit.

In the early years after being diagnosed with epilepsy, I had quite a few fits. They were a bit like a trip to the cinema in that they happened occasionally, although they were far from a treat. I always knew when one was starting in the same way that you know when you are going to be sick. In this crack of a time window, I would try to get help; I would shout to a family member, or if I was at school, I would tell my learning support assistant what was happening. And then the window would shut and the fit would start. During the furrows of fitting, I would tell my family that I was sorry and that I loved them. I never had any breathing problems when I had a fit, but the blind panic that it provoked in me felt like a bully was holding my head under water—I was desperately trying to shake loose and take some air into my lungs. During the fit I would be put into the recovery position, and Mum, Dad, and Simone's heads would bob in front of my face like buoys in the sea. Every time I had a fit, Simone was magnificent in how she would help my parents deal with the situation.

The most ill-timed fit occurred on Christmas Day one year. That was the worst Christmas of my childhood. I had a fit right after I had opened my presents. I was just about to play with my new knights and castle set when I was stopped in my tracks by the seizure. I was taken to the hospital and stuck on a ward populated by the children who were too sick to go home. I sat, watching death tease the patients. There was no Christmas cheer on that ward, just visions of the grim reaper lingering in the shadows. The day dragged, and missing my family was a given, but what I remember most about the day is that I lost the new Action Force figure that I had been given for Christmas and I missed watching *Star Wars Episode V: The Empire Strikes Back* on TV. I was very confused when *The Return of The Jedi* was shown the next Christmas, because I had no idea why Han Solo was a statue nor who Yoda was.

Over time, I came to realise life was going to be quite different. This realisation carried bitterness with it that I had yet to experience with having cerebral palsy. The impact of cerebral palsy had not yet come to the fore on a socially effecting level as far as I was concerned. I hadn't been rejected from the football team because of what I perceived to be my disability. I had not been turned down by a girl on account of my disability. I knew my cerebral palsy was there but it was like riding a bike with slightly flat tyres. The bike was still rideable, but it took more effort. Having epilepsy was different. I had to take medication to prevent myself having a fit. If I did not take the tablets, I ran the risk of having a fit.

I felt restricted. Out of nowhere, becoming a normal grown-up who could do normal things such as drink alcohol or drive a car (not at the same time mind you) were taken off the table. I was told that I wouldn't be able to go to discos because the flashing lights would send me spinning into a full-blown fit. It felt like doors were being shut and locked before I had been able to get up the doorsteps to ring the bell. I was a Jehovah's Witness having his nose broken by doors being slammed on him. My friends were having birthday parties at Laser Quest, and my mum had to turn down invites because the risk of me having a fit was too high. I felt like I was Peter Pan without the fun of flying and the gorgeous mermaids.

As far as I was concerned, the epilepsy had done something that the cerebral palsy had not done: it had stolen my future. Yes, cerebral palsy had altered the landscape of the future that lay ahead for me, but I had had no aspirations or preconceived ideas of how that future would be. By the time I was seven, I had imagined how my life would be, and now I had had a stranger come into my body and take my blueprints, as small and basic as they were, away. Maybe if the epilepsy had decided to make an appearance before I was capable of rational thought it might not have made as much of an impact as it did.

I haven't had a full blown fit since the early nineties. I sort of paralleled MC Hammer's pop career—I stopped having fits when he stopped having hits! My condition is very stable now—touch wood—and I have actually been able to do all of the things the doctors said I wouldn't be able to do except for drinking alcohol to excess. I drive, I go to nightclubs that have flashing lights, and shortly after my twenty-sixth birthday, I went to Laser Quest to complete my childhood. I still take tablets twice a day to control my epilepsy, and I wear a medical alert bracelet just in case the worst happens. I suppose, like the other conditions that I have, epilepsy has just become part of who I am, and I just get on with things the best I can with the help of my family, medication, and doctors.

9

THE SHORT STRAW

In a nightclub where the lights are dim and the music is loud, you have one perspective. You will be talking to a person and you may only understand one word out of every three they say due to the thudding music. The dim light distorts the image in front of you. In days gone by, before the smoking ban, your eyes had to fight against the fog of cigarettes. As the DJ plays the last song and tells everyone to leave, most of the revellers don't go just yet. Then the lights come on and everything looks different. People blink as eyes adjust to the light. Dark corners become fully lit open spaces. You turn to the girl you have been talking to and realise it is a man with long hair (okay, it happened once). People slow down when the lights come on; it is as if people in the club are prisoners making a run for it, and when the lights come on, they freeze. My perception of my childhood was a little like this scene, and one night my dad turned the lights on and made everything look different.

I thought I had extensive knowledge about my childhood, but I had memorised the abridged version of the story. I knew the main plot well—twenty-six minutes stillborn and so forth—but I had not looked at the bigger picture or paid attention to all the subplots and intricacies that come with a tale of such magnitude. At some time or another, we all have watched a film and not picked up on little details that make up the big picture. You walk away thinking, *I know what happened,* but then you talk to a friend who provides an explanation that makes you retract your statement and think, *I didn't get that at all*. The next day you find yourself watching the film again, trying to catch everything you missed. My moment where I had to rewind the film and watch again was when I interviewed my dad as part of a GCSE coursework essay.

The brief for the essay was to write about childhood experiences, and I had to talk to Dad in order to gather some facts that would bulk up the piece a bit. I had a list of questions about my childhood and about what my parent's hopes were for me. I think I managed to ask just one of the questions before Dad stopped me and cast the questions aside like a litterbug throwing a chocolate bar wrapper into the wind. He began a monologue, which thinking back to that night, conjures up images of a politician who tosses out the agenda and speaks from the heart. That is probably not a good example, as how often does that happen apart from when Hugh Grant played the prime minister in the film *Love Actually*? Nevertheless, the words pierced like a needle popping a balloon.

Dad talked about how the normal clichéd ambitions that parents harbour for their child were flung into the distance when I was born. Out of the window went hopes of me growing up to be a successful professional such as a solicitor or a CEO of a blue chip company. Thrown from the moving wagon were aspirations that I would reign supreme in a sports arena. All the parts of life's vehicle were stripped away, and what was left was the determination and will to keep the little engine running. My parents' only hope for me was that I would keep on breathing. Having a disabled child gave my parents clarity of what was important in my life.

When I asked Dad about his proudest memory of me as a child I expected him to wax lyrical about something monumental, but what I got instead evoked a feeling of absolutely humility. His answer was that he was most proud when I drank from a straw for the first time.

What can you say to that answer? The only thing I could do was grab the glass he offered me, which was filled to the brim with clarity, and drink from it. As I listened to Dad talk about how trivial accomplishments brought as much pride as bigger ones, I felt as if I had been brought out of a trance. Most people, including me up until that night, take for granted the trivial, almost inconsequential, acts that make up our day-to-day routines. It wasn't until I was given a glance into my life through the eyes of my dad that I understood the real achievements behind such non-events. I never knew I had struggled with sucking from a straw and to realise this put me in my place a bit. I was like most teenagers, caught up in the self-importance of striving to be popular and getting good exam results, but Dad took me out of my tunnel-vision landscape and showed me that even painting the big picture starts with basic strokes. Dad's awe-inspiring speech brought me to tears. They were not tears of sadness—they were tears brought about by the truth.

Fine motor skills that can be done in a blink of an eye by so many people are more difficult for me. As a child, my handwriting was illegible, and as an adult it is only mildly better. The shake in my hand is as if someone is nudging me while I write. Sometimes my penmanship looked more like a brainwave print out from an ECG machine. I had to learn how to find a way around such obstacles. The cure for my poor handwriting came with the advancement of technology. It became clear that my handwriting wasn't ever going to improve, thus my school provided me first with an electric typewriter and then a laptop for me to do my work.

Most able-bodied people will not think anything about filling up a glass of water from the tap. My cerebral palsy has not afforded me such a luxury. The whole process can feel like playing an arcade game where the target keeps moving. The old trusted trial-and-error strategy comes to the fore in these situations. I had tried placing the cup in the sink and then positioning the tap over it to fill it up, but the method that my hands took to more naturally was to place one finger over the tap in order to steady my hand and restrict my shaking as the glass filled.

Another example would be that instead of trying to pick the foil off a milk bottle that the milkman (remember those?) delivered, I would push my thumb down on the middle of the cap which would allow me to take it off easier. In school, I had peculiar scissors that I used; instead of the normal method of using scissors, I operated these by squeezing them in my fist like you would a stress ball. I still have them, although the blades are now rather blunt.

Eating has been another challenge for me throughout my life. When I was young, we had a crash barrier that surrounded my plate. It was like the wall that closes in the cars on a stock-car track; regularly, my cutlery would crash into the side as I tried to lure food on to my spoon and take the unpredictable journey to my mouth. I even had a mat that stuck my plate to the table just in case it fled the scene. I didn't use a knife for a long time, and I had to be persistent in catching the carrot at the end of my fork rather than the end of a stick. Even now, I have my imperfections. My clothes horse is currently drying a white T-shirt that has a big reddish-orange stain on it. There will always be spills when my hands have their own dance—it is as if they are body-popping towards my mouth. In these circumstances, I remember the night with Dad and the straw while quoting the Oasis song, 'Little by Little', 'Sweet perfection has to be imperfect.'

There is something spiritual in finding out something positive that you didn't know about your life. It's as if some blanks have been filled in, and you feel more aware of the road you have come from. The night Dad told me about sucking from the straw has stayed with me for over a decade. I still lose sight of my shaky beginnings, but when I refocus, I am given great insight into how far I have travelled.

The quote is 'The truth will set you free,' and in my case, it gave me a perspective that I had previously not had. I was fifteen when I had this conversation with my dad, and at that age I had blinkers on—all I saw was what was wrong with my life and what I couldn't do rather than what I could do. It was purifying for such revelations to be imparted to me. It was as if Dad had taken a pressure washer and blasted deep stains off my life's window. As the clean water dripped down, the window I was left with gave a clearer view of the mountains that I had scaled and the pitfalls I had negotiated.

I heard that in a public swimming pool, the surface of the water harbours all kinds of scummy substances that make the water unclear, and the same applies to the bottom of the pool. The only clean and clear water in a public swimming pool is in the middle between these two dirty areas. Speaking to Dad that night was as if he grabbed my hand and guided me to the middle layer of the swimming-pool lasagne. I could see clearly for the first time—my perceptions and memories were not clouded by murky waters any longer.

Sometimes it is hard to take stock of my achievements, because life's tide sweeps me off my feet and carries me away. I do try to make time to sit and look out of the window that Dad cleaned for me that night. Prominent in the view of how far I have come is a glass with a straw.

10

SIXTEEN BALLOONS

We'd been blowing up balloons for sixteen years. The doctors said I wouldn't live beyond the age of sixteen, so each year was akin to blowing up another balloon and adding it to the bunch in our hand. The more balloons we blew up, the more our feet were lifted off the ground. We held the balloons in our hands and dreamt that one day we'd fly away from the big number sixteen that we were standing on.

Like blowing up balloons, some years were harder than others. Some years knocked so much wind out of you that it was difficult to carry on. There were years we had to draw deeper breaths in order to conjure up enough effort to complete the year. Each year presented different obstacles to navigate, such as having fits or starting a new school. When I was young, I didn't know that the age sixteen was stalking my life, but my parents did. The situation must have seemed quite foreboding for them, wondering whether my life's lease would run out.

I can understand why Dad encouraged my adventurous spirit and tried to go with me on that roller coaster. That has a double meaning, because if I was at the fair, I would want to go on every roller coaster, but my life was a roller coaster too, with thrills and spills at every sharp turn. Dad wanted me to live life to the fullest in case the doctor's prognosis for me was true. I can flip the coin over and see my mum's view of what she wanted. Mum wanted to nurture me through the first sixteen years. She did not want to lose me to the sixteen-year guillotine that had designs on my life. Mum wanted to let me live, but she also wanted to protect me from danger. She had normal mother instincts to protect me, but she seemed to have had them spiked with 'Spidy senses' a la *Spiderman* that gave them an extra acuteness.

Negotiating pitfalls never got easier. We became more adept at bobbing and weaving, but a hammer blow would always come along to wobble us. The dangers we could see coming did not stun us as much as those we had not foreseen—those were the ones that knocked us over. There is no place for a glass jaw when you are dealing with a disability. My family developed a chin made of granite early on in my life. The cerebral palsy rocked us back, and the epilepsy knocked us over, but we had to get up and keep fighting. I am looking at my first sixteen years retrospectively and identifying a fighting resolve, but what I am describing now, at that time, was just life.

My daily existence was decorated with hospital appointments. They started with my parents' hunt for answers when they realised I wasn't as I should be, and they carried on throughout my first sixteen years. I would have to walk in a straight line so that the doctors could assess my balance, which was not achievable for all the will in the world. I would have to touch my nose and then touch the doctor's finger that was held out in front of me. It sounds easy but it is not such a simple process when you are trying to carry out the task with the shaky hands of cerebral palsy! The whole exercise was more about not poking the good doctor in the eye than anything else.

I was such a strange case that I was even paid by the hospital to be a guinea pig for trainee doctors; I turned up, and the fledgling doctors would examine me and try to diagnose me. I would get be paid ten pounds for my services, but I should have also pushed for a commission payment for every time the doctors 'guessed' wrong. None were ever successful in their diagnoses; a few confidently declared that I was blind! Pimping my disability out might seem bizarre to you, but for me it was just part of a routine.

Years rumbled on, and as I got older, my parents told me about the doctor's prediction. I did not retreat into my shell. I thought that the doctors were misguided fools, which turned out to be quite an accurate assessment. At times, life can feel like a train; you are put on a course and the track or destiny will not let you stray from the course that has been chosen for you. Time went by, and my mind's eye seemed to be coming into focus. I could see a station in the distance. This was the last stop on the route, and I would be able to get off and decide where I went from there. After that stop, all predictions would be deemed invalid, and I would be free. The train was our life, the tracks were our destiny, and the station was our freedom.

As the days, weeks, and months tumbled down off the calendar, they seemed to be burying the doctor's deathly prediction as we ambled along towards my sixteenth birthday. I started telling my friends that I was like a Duracel bunny, because just like those plucky, pink, battery-powered advertising icons, I just kept on going.

About the same time that I was coining the Duracel bunny joke, I was sitting in a science lesson, and Adam McGeever was holding court on our table. You could never really be sure whether Adam was being blasé or sincere when he decided to talk about subjects that everyone had an opinion on. He had and still has a tendency to play devil's advocate, and on this day he said that he didn't feel birthdays were as important anymore. I said that personally every birthday meant something to me because I wasn't supposed to live passed sixteen. I felt as if every birthday was another step towards proving the doctors wrong. Adam rolled his eyes and made a 'Oh, not again!' comment. Now that we are older, and we have a celebratory joke about my birthday, one of us will say 'ten years in the bonus rounds' or 'ten years living on borrowed time.' I find the jokes funny, but I stop from time to time and say 'Wow, this wasn't in the script. I'm ad-libbing now.'

Valuing each birthday as important was a shared feeling, and my parents planned holidays to see in such milestones in a way that befitted the moment. My sixteenth birthday was a monumental moment, and so my family and I went to Portugal with eight other family friends to celebrate what my sixteenth birthday meant to us all.

Reaching sixteen was like taking the shackles off me and releasing my family from the confined quarters in which they had operated. There is a picture of me on my sixteenth birthday that sits on a shelf in Mum's living room. It was taken just after I had told my mum how much of an achievement reaching sixteen was. I am still caught by a certain feeling of awe when I think about what we all overcame together to get to that birthday.

On my sixteenth birthday, my parents brought sixteen balloons into my hotel room and wished me happy birthday.

I'm sure it wasn't as symbolic as this chapter has made it out to be, but in the late afternoon we untied each one of the balloons and let them take flight from our balcony. Letting those balloons fly away was like letting go of the life expectancy. Dad filmed the balloons on his video camera as they meandered around the sky. The filming finishes with Dad focusing in on a girl in the distance walking hand-in-hand with a parent—in her other hand the girl is holding one of my balloons, and then the Portuguese sun sets.

I will always associate balloons with letting something go. I still hang on to the memory of what I have released into the sky, but for me, the release has a symbolic importance. Carrying around baggage is never easy, and I have learnt to apply what we did on my sixteenth birthday to other areas of my life. I symbolically let balloons of regret or anger float into the atmosphere. At least that is my aim; I am not always successful in letting every issue go, but who is? There are always challenges to face or balloons to blow up, but when the challenge has been met and slain, the balloons can be let go.

My sixteenth birthday will always be one of the most important days of my life. It was a juncture in my life but we were far from home free. New obstacles laid in wait, but on April 10, 1982, I was sixteen, and we were free.

Sixteen years, sixteen balloons.

11

LIVING ON THE WHITE SIDE OF DAD

Dad left our family home on October 8, 1999, to take part in a work golf day and never came back. He died of a massive heart attack on the fourteenth green of Middleton Hall Golf Course, which is near Kings Lynn in the county of Norfolk. There were no meaningful goodbyes or warnings, just a gaping hole in our family.

When my granddad on my mum's side died, the Dr Hook song 'A Little Bit More' was playing on the radio, and as we drove away from Kings Lynn where Dad's body lay, I saw a poster saying Dr Hook would be performing in Kings Lynn. I thought that was a sign that my granddad had come to collect my dad. Because the deaths had a little footnote that linked them together, the instances felt connected. In truth, they were separate random events, but the human soul does not think, and I was provided with a slender moment of solace.

The trees died that day. The rain stained the road a shade of black. Everything seemed to cast off any beauty, and the world became a dingy place. The feeling around his death seemed to be schizophrenic: there was an air of disbelief that Dad had died, but at the same time it was believable because it was incredibly real. He was not ever going to come through our front door again. He was never going to slap his hand on a door and hold his nose pretending that he had walked into it. He was never going to pour a can of beer into our gravy to give it a bit of flavour and then turn the wooden spoon upside down and launch into his rendition of Sweet's 'Blockbuster' or Mud's 'Tiger Feet'. The days didn't fly by; instead, they lingered. We were driftwood after a shipwreck, and I soaked the grief up.

Every splinter of my metaphorical piece of wood was immersed in the grief that flowed over me. I had so much grief travelling through my veins that if I had been weighed at the time I'm sure I would have been five stone heavier than I physically was. I lived in the past by replaying memories of Dad in my brain. They were always good memories, and they served me like shelter from the elements. If I insulated myself with my recollections, I would be safe from the immediate pain that waited for me at the door. I put together my personal Jim Maloney highlight reel so that he could stay with me.

I would remember him teaching me how to dive into a swimming pool, and more funnily, how we threw a horrid cousin of the family into the water and dive-bombed him even though he couldn't swim. You may gasp and say, 'Oh, that is awful', but the boy was a bully, and it felt like a victory. We were united against an evil, and we were teaching him not to mess with us. That is how it appeared to me. In those instances, I felt stitched together with my dad. It was us against the world.

I would think about our last summer together, when I worked for him at his cleaning company. I finally understood why he would fall asleep so early at night—he worked so hard. I saw that he enjoyed his job, but the main reason he worked was to give his family a comfortable lifestyle, and I really respected that about him. It made me want to model myself after Dad, at least in a professional sense. I wanted people to link me to Dad, 'Oh, that's Jim's son; aren't they alike?'

Dad had a temper, and I even allowed myself to glamorize his behaviour. 'My, my, he did have a temper. Wasn't it funny?' But it wasn't funny. I bent and shaped my image of Dad to fit my grief and the result was that he became my saint. That is not to say this is not a common reaction to someone dying. All of a sudden, the person was everyone's best friend and was prone to such acts of kindness that Mother Teresa would be put in the shade. This seems to happen whether it is warranted or not. I suppose it may have something to do with the sentence, 'You cannot speak ill of the dead.'

I subscribed to this stance for nearly a decade. My dad was the man who motivated me; he made me the man I have become. He's the reason I am here. I worshipped him, and I treated his failings like the quality streets sweets that I didn't like: I buried them and chose the ones that tasted good. My outlook on Dad must have rankled Mum, because I sort of downplayed her role in how I was raised. I reasoned that she had cared for me, but Dad had *made me*, which was only half the story. Their efforts were equal. Mum was strong enough to break free from the party line and say, 'No, no, no, he was not a saint by any means!' Mum would tell me the negative things about Dad that I was blacking out like key sentences on a top-secret document released to the public. I didn't like it. I was angry that she would desecrate the memory of the great Jim Maloney.

Elisabeth Kubler-Ross was a psychiatrist who was a shining light in the field of near-death studies. Her most famous work is arguably the Kubler-Ross model that identifies and explains the five stages of grief. They are denial, anger, bargaining, depression, and acceptance. The principle is that a grieving person will go through each stage as they come to terms with their loss. Each stage is interchangeable, for example, a person may go from denial to bargaining and back again before they move on to another stage. There is no predetermined timeframe in which a person goes through the stages.

For a long time I was stuck in the depression stage. I missed Dad, and I didn't want to get on with life. My depression supplanted my cerebral palsy and made itself the high king of my disabilities. I was paralysed by my loss. I shed a lot of tears and found comfort in photos and songs that reminded me of Dad. Anything I did was soured because I couldn't tell my dad about it. Mobile phones were just becoming the juggernaut industry that they are now and the revolution of texting had started. I would look at my mobile and think *I'm never going to text Dad, 'How R U?'* Working for Mum in the company that Dad built was to be surrounded by him; to clean a floor with a buffing machine was to relive him showing me how to use it.

The depression lasted at least two years. I finally came out of that stage and started putting together a life. However, I now realise that I built that life firmly in the field of bargaining. To be closer to Dad and to honour him I modelled myself on him. The decisions that I made were second-guessed by the question 'What would Dad do?' If I made a mistake, I would chastise myself and say, 'Dad would never make that mistake.' If I could be like Dad, I bargained that he was still alive inside of me.

Every one of my achievements was linked to Dad. Dad was in the back of my car helping me when I passed my test. Dad was in the corner of the room giving me a head nod if I kissed a girl. I learned to window clean despite my hands shaking, but it wasn't my achievement, it was dedicated to Dad. I became like a footballer who dedicates every goal to his dead parent. The ironic thing is that that behaviour drives me crazy: Okay, point to the sky and bow your head the first time you score after the death, but then that should be it. Do you really think someone who sells insurance gets off the phone after finalising a deal and says, 'That's for you, Dad/Mum!'? And yet, I had become that person.

If I tried to work through a difficult patch in a relationship, it was because Dad never walked away from Mum. When I dated multiple women and slept with a fair few, it felt really good, but part of me was doing it because Dad told me when I was a teenager that that was what dating was all about. I wanted to be like my dad told me he was like when he was single: a lady killer.

I would compare Dad's success in the business world and with money to my success or failures. I wasn't dealing in actualities however; I was dealing with my perceptions. My mum told me that he had run up a lot of credit card debt just before he died, and so he wasn't quite as financially savvy as I made him out to be in my head, but even then he was a beacon of glamour because he took some risks, and I decided that they paid off usually. He was quite literally my life; he lived on through me, and although I didn't think I could match up to him, I didn't want to make even one crack in his perfect memorial.

I personally thought I was at the stage of acceptance, and in some regard I was. I had accepted that Dad was gone and that I would never see him again, thus I had grappled and come to terms with reality. But I wasn't living in reality. For one thing, I had made Dad into this perfect person that he wasn't, and for another, I was living my life as if he was governing my every decision. That is not acceptance of what happened, but merely an effort to sculpt Dad into a memory that I was comfortable with.

For nine years I had chiselled Dad into this mystical figure that I saw as the most flawless father to ever walk on earth. However, whilst I was writing this book, I started to remember unsavoury things about my father that conflicted with the esteem I held him in. I was back in the depression stage of grief, but this time I was dealing with two deaths. The death of the father I had built up in my head and the death of the father I actually had. I was at odds with myself. I felt betrayed by myself and betrayed by my father.

Things are rarely black and white. We live our lives in the grey most of the time. My reactions to Dad dying fixed the spotlight firmly on to the white side, glorifying him. I could say that that led me to build my life on half a story, and I could reprimand myself for doing that, but Dad did raise me very well and the qualities in him that were good were very good such as morals, respect, and loyalty. Furthermore, I had not made up all the good memories that I had focused on. I do feel so blessed to have so many good memories of my dad. However, I had obscured the whole picture, and that meant when I uncovered it all, I couldn't handle the truth.

I went through hell emotionally when the rose-tinted glasses fell off my face. The light hurt my eyes as they readjusted. Dad had to become a demon before I could bring him back into my heart. However, when he came back to me, he was fuller and well-rounded—and a human being rather than having the image of a Greek god. In the words of the band Embrace, I had to 'Come back to what you know/Take everything real slow/I wanna lose you but I can't let you go.' And I suppose that was the whole point. I had to slowly rebuild my memories of Dad and come back to what I knew, because he will always be part of me, and I will never let him go.

12

Living with the Dark Side of Dad

My early childhood Sunday memories are populated with the same people. Caroline, Bozey, Hayley, and Kim Wilmer would join Mum, Dad, Simone, and me in filling the time on the Lord's day. We seemed to be a band of adventurers, drawn together initially by Mum and Caroline who had been best friends at school.

Our days together would be filled with children giggling and adults laughing. We went on holidays together in trailer-tents and caravans. We ate Dad's burnt barbeque and wondered if all food cooked this way tasted as bad as what Dad served up. Dad's sausages looked as if they were fingers from a charcoaled corpse, and I daresay they tasted similar.

We used to pile into two cars and drive in convoy to a garden centre to spend a few hours sifting through the greenery. We children mostly occupied ourselves on the playgrounds. One day we were on the way back from Baytree Garden Centre, which is situated in the fenland countryside of Lincolnshire about forty-five minutes away from Peterborough. I was about five years old at the time. Suddenly excitement reigned in the car: an airplane was flying in the cloudy, overcast, white sky.

This particular day we were all in just one car, as Bozey hadn't come with us. Mum and Dad implored everybody to look up into the sky to see the plane. I was stirred by my parent's animation, and I became very anxious to see the plane. I could hear its loud engine chugging away but I couldn't see it. My eyes began to dart frantically around the sky as I desperately tried to find the plane. Since I have become an adult, I have felt the same irrational impulse flow through my veins when I am already late and I can't find my keys. I was stuck on the back seat convinced I was missing out on the best thing that I would ever see. The frustration was tearing at my insides and thus I started to whine and shout 'Where is it? I can't see it!' as I became ever the more frustrated at my inability to see the plane that was no doubt made out of gold and had a dragon's tail.

On and on I went: 'Where is it? I can't see it! Where is it? I can't see it! Where is it? I can't see it!' Until, out of nowhere, Dad slammed on the brakes and the car stopped in the middle of the road.

The next thing I was aware of was being held in the air outside of the car by Dad's big hands. Then there was a smash, and I was looking up at Dad's face from the bonnet. Dad cast a shadow over me that felt as dark as the darkest night. The air was cold but the hot engine underneath me and the searing heat that burnt inside me combined to make a pressure cooker environment as I tried to comprehend what was going on. Tears rolled off my cheeks on to the car, and then Dad shook me. He shouted into my face, *'Can you see it now? Eh? Can you see it now?'*

With an urgency that I had never known in my five years, I searched the sky for the plane, but all I could see was my dad's face and hair. I made a mistake. I answered 'No' because I still longed to see the plane that was probably gone by this stage. Dad shook me again and shouted repeatedly, *'Can you see it now? Eh? Can you see it now?'* By this point, my eyes were nothing but a tsunami of tears, and I had no chance of seeing anything, let alone the fabled plane. I muttered 'Yes' to Dad's question, although I had not seen the plane, and I was put back in the car. The ride home resumed and took place under a blanket of silence for the remainder of the trip.

That is my first recollection of being gripped by pure terror by my dad's behaviour. I was absolutely petrified. I had been confronted by a man who looked like my father but did not act as my father. There was a fury in his eyes that I had never encountered, and it burnt right through me.

My dad kept secrets about his childhood experiences that played havoc within him. I believe that my helplessness, and the frustration he felt about not being able to address this, triggered a memory from his past that led him to act the way he did on that country road. The problem about that last sentence is that I have written it as an adult, who is capable of rational thought. However, at the time, I was still a few years away from the recognised commencement of rational thought in a child's mind. I did not grasp that the plane was not one of a kind and that I would see a different plane at another time. And I did not have the capacity to rationalise that I may have stirred up emotions in Dad during our ill-fated pointing game of 'look up at the plane'. At the time, I was scared to my wits' end.

Sometimes I would play up, as a child will occasionally do. I may have been rude about the food put in front of me, used a swear word, or made a demand for pizza at six o'clock in the morning at an airport. At times, I was rude to my mum or sister. My behaviour rarely strayed out of the box that would define normal child indiscretion, but Dad had a short temper and sometimes, not always, he would leap to being very angry rather than taking steps forward in a more rational manner.

At times Dad could be violent. He was absolutely sensational when explaining elements of my disability to me. However, he was not nearly as adept at expressing what was going on inside of him. His father had not been the most approachable of men. To see him, Dad would have to make an appointment. Dad had been sent away to boarding school when he was six, which meant that he never learnt any parenting skills from his father.

Dad was a very complex character, who had many demons. He never confronted these demons, and I never knew about the extent of his emotional scarring from childhood while he was alive. Indeed, Mum only found out the magnitude of Dad's psychological childhood trauma the night before he died.

My grandparents did not tell my dad that he was going to boarding school. They packed up his things and told him they were going for a day trip. When they got to the school, they took Dad and his things in with them and then they disappeared. My dad went outside looking for his parents but found that the car had gone. Dad sat on the steps outside the boarding school for hours waiting for them to come back and take him home, but they didn't return.

Dad tried to run away from the boarding school several times because he was so unhappy there. His parents finally took him out of the school, but they kept sending Dad away to other schools, which must have made him feel as though he didn't have a home and wasn't wanted.

In a stroke or serendipity, Dad had disclosed a lot about his past to Mum the night before he died. This seems surreal; it was as if Dad knew that that would be his last chance to tell Mum about his childhood. I am not going to share more than I have with you regarding his history because it does not feel right. I feel that I would be betraying him if I were to do so. I will say that what he disclosed that night shed some light on why he had such a short temper.

There is a difference between excusing someone's behaviour and seeing a reason for that behaviour. I do not excuse my dad's behaviour, but I do try to find reasons for it in order to understand what happened and to move on. I must say, understanding the reasons behind Dad's actions is a lot easier than just thinking about the behaviour—when these things happened to me I was very scared and confused.

Dad had a high-risk parental strategy from very early on in my life. He would say to Mum, 'I don't care if Stuart hates me, but I will make him the best he can be.' Knowing that in hindsight, gives me some comfort in that I can see that Dad's intentions were good; it was his methods that were extreme and at times inappropriate. I am overwhelmed by what I perceive to be an act of self-sacrifice on my dad's part. He was willing to forego a relationship with me in exchange for making me the best I could be. However, playing the tough father sometimes led to the lines becoming blurred. Sometimes the hard line that Dad struck did not end with the disability. It was as if he played the tough role for so long that residue seeped into other areas of our lives, such as what happened with the plane incident.

Dad used to help me with my maths homework every Sunday. Sunday, how I hated that day! I am relatively good at maths; I will never be a maths genius, but I get by. The reason why I failed maths twice was that although I knew how to work out the maths problem, I had to dictate the process to another person. Trying to articulate my mathematical thinking to a second party became a too long of a linguistic bridge and confusion would jump on to the page.

Each time Sunday came around, my incomprehensible instructions would frustrate Dad, and the tension would build. Sensing this, panic would spread throughout my body till my mind was sending answers out of my mouth I knew were wrong. Dad would then become angry and shout at me. I didn't respond well to his shouting, and I would cry. By the time Sunday dinner rolled round, the friction would have spread through the house, and the simmering atmosphere was palpable. It wasn't unknown for Dad to get mad at me while we were at the dinner table. On occasions, I would be stopped from eating so he could make me hold a heavy gravy jug out in front of me while I recited my times tables. I was not allowed to put the jug down until I got the times tables right. It was a torture technique, because as the pain built in my arms I would shake more. I'm sure he derived no pleasure from such measures, but that doesn't make a difference.

Dad forced my head down the toilet once and told me if I didn't start working at school I would 'end up cleaning these' for the rest of my life. The tactic worked but not because it scared me. I worked hard and passed the exams I needed to because I wanted to prove the 'bastard' wrong. Dad knew this was what inspired me to do well, and I think he was prepared to sacrifice our relationship for my long-term future. It was a gamble that had side effects, because it convinced me that he didn't like me.

While Dad had me in a grip of chaos, Mum would be there pleading for him to stop treating me that way. Mum would beg, 'Jim, please stop it! Jim, please!' But Dad was usually in a place of such temper that he could hear nothing but his own thoughts. Mum is such a loving, nurturing mother, and the sight of her son being treated in this manner was as if she was being speared through the heart with an oak tree. Dad's treatment of me was abusive, and as a result it drove a wedge between my parents for quite some time. I feel a gritty monster rubbing my stomach lining with his rough skin when I think about being a bone of contention between the two. They were so good together, but different approaches to situations can cause a lot of damage. My mum did try to stop him from treating me badly, but there were destructive influences in Dad that he still kept secret at that point.

During this time, it was easy to see Dad as demonic because our relationship was predominantly unpleasant. Viewing Dad in such a way made our relationship very tenuous and fragile in my adolescent mind. All positivity that existed between Dad and I was disappearing from view. Our relationship, from my perspective, was like the straw house that the first of the three little pigs made in the fairy tale. All it took was for the wolf to come along and start to blow, and the house fell down. That moment came one evening when I was fourteen, when Dad conjured up the big wolf-generated gust of air that blew away any positive feelings about him that remained in my head. He blew my house down, and anything good I felt about him took flight; the only thing I had left to protect me was a blanket of negativity that I wrapped myself in.

Having no social life to speak of as a fourteen-year-old, I had little option but to accompany my parents and sister to a family friend's house one Saturday evening. Whilst we were there, Dad was involved in a discussion about early parenthood. I was positioned next to him on the most comfortable leather couch I had ever sat upon, totally unprepared for the revelation Dad was about to drop into my lap.

His tone of voice was so nonchalant, his body language was so relaxed, and the words tripped off his tongue in such a blasé manner, that one would be forgiven for thinking he was discussing the weather. But what he actually said was this:

'Stuart had been crying every night for eighteen months. I was up with him one night, and as I was trying to stop him from crying, I faced a wall. I was so frustrated with him that I turned him upside down and got ready to smash him against the wall. I swear, if he hadn't stopped crying when I turned him upside down, I would have killed him!'

I felt as if I had been punched in the stomach and then had a steel chair smashed on my head. I was dazed by this admission. My dad loved me so; how could he ever contemplate killing me? I couldn't comprehend what he was saying. What made it worse was how carefree he seemed as he told his story. He was ripping out my heart and stamping on it over and over, but he was telling the anecdote in such a matter-of-fact way. I was dumbfounded.

My opinion of my father changed greatly for the next few years. The wall story was the final nail in the coffin; I was convinced by that chilling account, and the other extreme acts, that my dad was evil. I hated him for contemplating murdering me; I couldn't understand how he could do that. What I did understand was that he could be violent towards me, so with my teenage logic I determined he was capable of killing me.

To say that Dad and I healed our rift whilst he was alive would be inaccurate; I never brought up the subject again after that night. I don't even know if he was aware of the pain he caused me. We did get on better for the last eighteen months of his life, probably partly because he stopped helping me with my maths homework. I filed 'Wallgate' somewhere and forgot where I put it.

The human mind is a fantastic specimen. It is like a library in a way, because it stacks memories away like books on a shelf. It can also be like a gravedigger: it literally digs a hole for a memory or two and then buries them. The memories stay buried until one day you stumble over a dip and realise you're standing on a shallow grave. The next thing you know you have uncovered a buried memory. I have experienced both of these similes whilst writing this book. I had not thought about Dad's 'wall' story for many years—until I sat down to write an anecdotal essay about how being hung upside down when I was younger helped my cerebral palsy (I don't know why or how this action helps with cerebral palsy), and the memory jumped out and hit me on the nose.

These memories inflicted pain on every particle of my body, and I was consumed by anger and sadness. I was angry that my dad would ever consider killing me, I was angry that he told the story, and I was angry at the book for leading me down this path of rediscovery. I felt a deep sadness, because the memory had come back to me too late. Dad had been gone for many years before this memory knocked on my brain's door. What use was it now? I couldn't confront Dad about the incident, but I couldn't forget the memory now. To me, it appeared to indicate that definitive closure to the whole affair was very unlikely.

I regret that I never discussed Dad's tale with him. It was a chest infection that I never treated with Benylin. If I had talked to Dad about the wall speech I would have gotten it off my chest, and my feelings towards my father might have been a little less complex. Unfortunately, this did not happen. He died, and I had to come to terms with the wall incident with the help of a counsellor.

Sometimes you go shopping for T-shirts and come back with jeans as well. After my first serious relationship broke up, I decided to seek counselling. Deep down, I knew I needed counselling about my dad, but the issues that were in the forefront of my mind were those that concerned my dissolved relationship. I think I was a car that had been fixed up admirably by my family and friends, but it had gotten to a stage where I needed a professional to take a look at me. Counselling cleared my mind of the toxic fumes that were choking me.

My counsellor and I were a bit like firefighters in that once we had finished putting out the fire of the issues with my ex, we started to tackle my problems with my dad.

We spent hours making sense of my relationship with my father. I always worried that he didn't like me because of how harshly he treated me. I was certain that Dad loved me, but I didn't believe he liked me. By working with my counsellor, I was able to see that sometimes people who are similar do not always get on. I could make peace with this because it was not a slight on either Dad or me. Adding this theory to Dad's declaration of 'I don't care if Stuart hates me, but I will make him the best he can be', I was able to understand some of Dad's behaviour towards me.

An exercise that my counsellor did with me brought some peace and closure regarding the whole wall affair.

The exercise was challenging, I had to assume several different roles in the memory and look at the incident from that perspective. I had to look at the situation from my fourteen-year-old self's perspective; then I had to take on the role of my dad at the time he was telling the story and describe his motives for telling our friends about this experience with me and how he felt while telling it. I had to speak in the first person and describe my feeling as Dad.

I then had to 'be' Dad in the moment he was describing. I had to think as if I was my dad holding his son upside down looking at the wall. The exercise is not a complete science. I will never really know what my dad was truly thinking on the night he hung me upside down or on the night that he told the story in front of me, but I was able to gain a different perspective about the event.

From trading roles in the exercise, I was able to see that Dad did not hate me but he did hate the situation. I had been crying every night for eighteen months, and my parents had not had a good night's sleep in that time. Nerves were frayed, and not knowing why I was crying added frustration to a situation that was a potential powder keg. Dad was experiencing the same helplessness that he felt when his parents had left him at the boarding school. He had no answers, and that is what drove him to breaking point. In a moment of madness, he realised he could take back control in a situation that had been slipping out of his grip for some time. I saw the incident through Dad's eyes for the first time, and although it may not have necessarily been his view, it gave me an understanding of what happened that night.

The last part of the exercise involved me being a time traveller who arrives at that moment to give advice to Dad just as he looks at the wall. The exercise allowed me to step into that dark space that I imagine in my mind and say to

Dad 'It is not your fault and it is not Stuart's fault. He is hurting. He is not sleeping because he has cerebral palsy, not because you are missing something.' This may sound stupid, but I did feel I was laying the incident to rest as I was visualising talking to Dad in the exercise. I was in possession of the facts, and Dad wasn't. He had no light at the end of the tunnel, whereas I was looking back from the light into the tunnel from the other side.

How do I feel now about my father's actions? I understand him and his reasons a lot better than when I was fourteen. I shudder when I think of some of his antics, but I believe that he was a flawed individual trying his best. His methods were at times well within the realms of insanity, and I can't condone the times when they spilled out and turned into actual cruelty. But I can respect his end goal. I feel sad that he died before we could settle our issues. I often fantasize about seeing him again and being able to ask him if the sacrifice was worth it. My mum told me that towards the end of his life he admitted that he did regret how badly he treated me, but he would say: 'I did it to make him the best he could be.'

So where am I now concerning my feelings about my dad? I do not think he should be paraded around on the shoulders of saints, nor do I believe he should be cast down to wherever the villains of our time go. I have put the rose-tinted glasses in a drawer, and I have hung up my bat that I beat up Dad's memory with. What I am left with is a memory of a real man. If it was a picture, different parts would blur into one, and yet it maintains a clear focus. I see my father for what and who he was, and that has charm in itself. I am not blinded by an obligation to worship or an impulse to jump to hate.

There are people in this world who, for whatever reason, needed to be raised with a strong hand, and they didn't get one. As a consequence, they fell into bad ways or didn't make as much of themselves as they possibly could or should have. Dad felt that he needed to be tough on me in order for me to be able to live rather than just exist in life. For this, I will always be grateful. I wish the abusive behaviour hadn't happened, but we can't change the past. I will never forget the problems I had with my dad but I have to accept what I cannot change and move on.

The dad I remember today is very different to the dad I dressed up to be perfect after his death, and that works for me. I feel no guilt for acknowledging how he hurt me, which I think is healthy. And, as for the good times we had, I thank him for the memories.

I believe this is what the fifth stage of grief is for me. My acceptance is that I accept Dad for everything he was and still is to me. I will always love him, and he will always be a big part of my life, but I can move on from the grief now without his memory weighing me down and with a balanced picture of the man.

13

<u>SIMONE</u>

My earliest memory is of my sister. I was playing in the nursery section of the school playground, which was cordoned off by fencing so the toddlers didn't get lost. The fence had gaps between the individual planks of wood where it was possible to look out and see the rest of the pupils running around. Simone came to one of the breaks in the fence to talk to me. She pressed her face up against the wood and asked about my day. I can still see her soft face talking to me in an animated way. Simone and I are different people with our own strengths and weaknesses and our own personalities, but this snippet of a memory strips away everything, and what remains is a show of love between two siblings.

Mum's earliest memory of Simone interacting with me is when my sister was brought to the hospital by her godmother, Paula. She was carrying a present for me that she was excited to give. A week later when I was brought home from hospital, Simone greeted me by throwing a hard ball at my head! That was the day the tough love started. Simone has never seen me as disabled. I have to begrudgingly give her a free pass on the fury that people incur from me when they approach me with this line of thought. By treating me with a harsh approach, she helped mould my character and make me as strong as I am today. I never really subscribed to Simone's assertion that she helped raise me, but if strengthening a sibling's character is not a method of raising them, I do not know what is. Even though the way she treated me was sometimes too harsh, I have to be grateful for the preparation for life she gave me.

Simone and I were a public interest story in the local paper when we were toddlers. The headline read 'Sister's Love Helps Brother Through', and part of the story focused on how Simone helped me overcome the obstacles placed in my way by the cerebral palsy. We posed for a picture on our garden swing, Simone was standing, and I was sitting in between her feet. Even though I found it hard to stay on the swing with Simone on it as well, we looked really happy together. Simone treated me as if I was able-bodied, but at the same time, when Mum and Dad needed her help, such as when I started having fits, she threw herself into the role. Simone would do anything to aid my parents when I was on the floor fitting. She would run and get suppositories or help keep me in the recovery position and out of harm's way. If there was any comfort for me during a fit, it was that my sister was there, and she would do whatever she could for my parents and me.

We did a lot of things together as a family when we were growing up. Some families go their own way, and it is a struggle from early on to get everybody together, but most weekends we would go to watch Peterborough United play football. We really should have picked a team that didn't subject us to such a barrage of ineptitude in terms of football quality, but we were all spending time together, which was the important thing.

Watching Peterborough play in the mid-nineties was like taking a tour of a sewage factory for the most part: the experience was not something you would recommend. One of the main elements in keeping our family going to the games was that it was a family ritual we enjoyed. What made the experience worthwhile were the quirks and little absurdities about match day. It was fun to watch the female steward who fancied Dad frisk him or have Mum frisked. Simone and I would enjoy making fun of the man who told us that we didn't sing enough. He would say that when he was young, he would shout out, *'Who takes the corner? Who takes the corner?'* After the aforementioned lecture, we took it upon ourselves to emphatically chant this at the appropriate time. Simone would use me as a windbreaker, which was such a comical liberty. All these oddities brought us together on most Saturdays.

It's hard watching your sister be the sport star. Simone played netball all the way up to county level; she also played tennis and hockey for her school. I had to stand and watch from the sidelines. I can look back and say honestly that I am proud of all of Simone's sporting achievements, but when we were younger, I confess that I desperately wanted to be the one excelling on the sporting fields. My eyes would glaze over slightly when watching my sister play sports; partly because of boredom, but also there was a little bit of jealousy at work in the pit of my stomach. I was searching for somewhere that I belonged. I wanted to be a part of a team like Simone was, but I just felt my insecurities magnify. I was a disabled boy struggling to find a social place. I was envious of Simone being a sporting insider when I believed I was an outcast in the sporting and social sense.

I first wrote this chapter under the impression that I felt resentment towards Simone for being such a sports star, but after a lot of soul searching I see the resentment was misplaced, as were my ambitions. I couldn't compete in able-bodied sports, but I could compete in games for the disabled. But at this stage in my life, I did not want to be labelled as disabled so therefore I had no sporting outlet, which just left me to look over at Simone playing sports with an envious eye.

I was carrying a bowl of self-resentment around, and occasionally it would morph into jealousy or anger. And then there would be an overspill and someone would end up with negativity being thrown his or her way. I didn't really resent Simone; I resented my disability, because I thought it was holding me back with regard to joining sports teams. My mind was narrower than a small country lane, because there are many able-bodied people who cannot get into sports teams because they have no ability let alone have a disability.

This sporting jealousy makes me ashamed when I see how proud Simone is of my sporting accomplishments. I won an award at school for Outstanding Achievement in Physical Education. I was in shock; I thought there had been some kind of mistake. I even asked my PE teacher if it was correct. When I was assured that I had been the most popular choice, I settled down to write some kind of end-of-term report. Simone came into the dining room where we were working, and I beckoned her over furiously. I bundled the letter into her hand and she read it. Simone literally jumped up and down on the spot and kissed me in front of all my classmates, but I didn't care. The thought of Simone being so proud of me makes me equally as proud to have her as a sister.

For a long time I have misconstrued the relationship that my sister and I share. I always took the view that we predominantly didn't get on throughout our years together. This was true, as many times we fought like cats and dogs. That is a behaviour pattern though and does not define our whole relationship. Simone came up with a better way to describe our at-times-edgy relationship: we bicker a lot. We were both raised to have opinions, and some of those views differed, which led to little skirmishes. Our family environment did suffer from a lack of harmony at times due to our bickering, and when Simone said something that hurt me I had a tendency to hold on to it. I am not a victim, and I can sting Simone with just as much force, but under the sniper fire, our family foundations are built from love.

I think that our verbal jousts carry a lot of sibling rivalry in them. At times, due to my disability, I have not felt equal, which leads me to fight harder in verbal battles with Simone in order to come out on top. I do try to keep this yearning in check, but my metaphorical hand sometimes struggles to put down the sword. Fighting for equality leads me to put my fists up when there is nothing to fight. I am not alone in the disabled community on that score. A lot of older people with disabilities are so used to fighting that they come out swinging from their corners when no one is in front of them. I am sometimes asked by my mum and my sister why am I fighting them on something, and quite a lot of the time, the reason is that it is in my nature. I have to try to keep calm and just say that Simone and I have different views and that is okay. I do not need to score any points. Life is a work of art—the day you stop creating and improving upon it is the day you die. Progress can be made; it just takes time.

Fathers have different relationships with their daughters than they do with their sons. I struggle with feelings of resentment towards Simone because I thought Dad was more lenient with Simone than he was with me. Simone seemed to always be well sheltered, and I always was in the eye of the storm when Dad would lose his temper. By the time I was having these feelings and asking these questions, Dad had died, thus I will never get an answer straight from the horse's mouth that would allow me to gulp down the pint of complete closure.

Sometimes my vision can be blinkered, and I struggle to see why Simone did not get punished to the extent that I did. What clouds the issue further is that we both misbehaved to similar levels. I know that Dad loved us very much, but what wasn't clear to me was whether Dad liked to be around me or not. I was envious of the relationship that Simone enjoyed with our father, but the dynamics were like a magic-eye picture that you have to step away from and take a second look. Fathers are often harsher with their sons. Throughout the ages, the man has always been seen as the hunter. Fathers can be harder on their male children so that their sons can become providers for their families. Whereas the daughters can be seen as their little girls, and since their daughters do not need to be taught how to hunt and survive, they are subjected to softer treatment.

Dad put a few more spicy ingredients into the hunting sauce that he used when marinating me, because he thought that I would need survival instincts that were far more acute. Dad foresaw a tougher slog for me because of my disability, which could have led to me being shaped more with sandpaper rather than being buffed to shine with a bit of polish and a soft cloth. Simone and I had different fatherly experiences and this caused tension sometimes. My experiences of Dad are more like a beautifully handcrafted, antique coffee table that has a few scratches here and there that have occurred over time.

Despite the contrasts in some of our experiences, Simone and I would do well to accept that we had two different relationships with Dad, and that is okay. We do not have to have exactly the same views of him. Simone can say he was her best friend, and I can say he was the dad I needed because he pushed me, yet sometimes he was cruel. Neither opinion impedes on the other's memory.

Simone and I visited Santa one year, and he gave us both tiny Christmas trees that we could grow in our garden. Dad planted them both and we sat back and watched. Unfortunately, Simone's grew fantastically well, and mine hardly made it out of the ground. The contrast in the two trees' development was so vast that there was a family joke that mine was disabled. I have to be honest and say that that did hurt, but I can see no better analogy to describe Simone and me. At times I looked at her tree and felt jealousy, but what was really going on was that I wasn't happy with the state of my tree. Growth came so easy to Simone's tree that I worried that mine would never catch up. But under closer inspection, both trees were as similar as they were different. They developed at different rates but their roots were the same. The difference in the size of their branches was vast, but they still had the same leaves. The trees were still part of the same family.

14

Pyjama Friends

Some friendships can feel uncomfortable, like a shirt with a collar that is too tight. The collar feels as if it has been starched so much that your neck cannot move for the stiffness. Movements become awkward because the garment enforces such a restriction. The collar cuts off your air supply, and the next thing you know you are gasping for gulps of fresh air. However, some friendships are like pyjamas. They are so comfortable that you take them everywhere with you. The pyjamas give you room to breathe, but you feel as though you are at one with them. Some friends are so relaxing to be around that it is like wearing your favourite pyjamas.

I have had both sides of the wardrobe. I didn't have many comfortable friendships when I was at secondary school. I tried to fit in with the perceived 'cool crowd' but I found myself trying to shoehorn myself into a space that was being closed. My place in this clique seemed to be fine for a while, but soon I felt as if I was the yellow puss in a spot that the group needed to squeeze out.

One lunchtime they gathered around me and took turns pushing me over with one finger. A feat they succeeded in due to my poor balance. All I could do was to reach out to grab hold of something to keep me upright. As I fell, I would launch my hands upwards to save myself, and what I found was the shirt pocket of the person who was pushing me. The pushing was so bad during one lunchtime that I ripped several pockets clean off of their shirts.

Another lunchtime these boys lured me off the school campus to a residential area that I was unfamiliar with. One minute I felt part of the group, the next minute they had run away from me. I didn't understand how I went from laughing and joking with them to trying in vain to catch up with them as they took flight. I was left all alone in an area I didn't know, and as I watched the group run away, it was as if my popularity was running away from me too. I felt very lonely as I tried to find my way back to the school grounds. It was hard to draw any conclusion other than that these boys found it funny to exploit my physical shortcomings by running off. The street was empty, and it felt as though it still had more friends than I did at that moment.

You could say, 'Okay, make friends with the other kids with disabilities.' However, that has never been quite so simple. When I was diagnosed with cerebral palsy, the hospital told my parents not to go in search for other families who also had a child with the same condition because I was different. I was not as severe, and I would not fit in. The words turned out to be quite prophetic.

My parents were founding members of a support group for families who had children with cerebral palsy. The group was called *Cerepal*, and again I was accepted in this social circle for a while, but once I began to progress both physically and mentally, things became difficult for my family. There was tension between the other members of Cerepal and my parents, which led to my family deciding to distance ourselves from the organisation.

The situation had a sad irony about it because Cerepal was set up to improve the lives of children with cerebral palsy. When I improved, the organisation shut us out. I suppose seeing me improve so much when other children were not must have ate at some of the parents and frustrated them as they hoped against hope that their children might catch up to me.

The frustration wasn't just one way; as I took strides towards a more mainstream existence, I found it harder to relate to the other children associated with cerebral palsy who were more severely affected than I was.

Sometimes I feel I am straddled over two tracks. At times, I have been too disabled for the able-bodied universe to really welcome me into their bosom, and on other occasions, I have not been disabled enough to be taken into the hearts of the disabled community. I didn't fit in on either side; I lived in a world of labels, and yet no one could decide what label I should wear.

Having experienced friendships that have made me feel isolated, I am able to appreciate the special friendships that have come into my life.

I believe that life lays out some friends for you to find along the way. You don't know when, where, or how you're going to meet them, but they are waiting for you somewhere down the road. I have been fortunate enough to encounter quite a few friends who I believe I was destined to meet. I could list them all here and now, but that may sound a bit like a thank-you speech. Instead, I am going to share with you how different friendships have been part of different stages of my life, and how they have shaped my development.

The first stage in my friendship metamorphosis was and always will be the Wilmer family. To me, they are as present as the stars in the sky and as constant as my own family—the Wilmer family have always been with me. For the first ten or so years of my life, our social calendars were woven together. Mum and Caroline had been friends since their school days, and Dad became best friends with Bozey, a bizarre nickname that stuck because when he broke his leg as a teenager he pulled a face that looked like one of the newsreaders of the time, Reginald Bozenquet.

Bozey and Caroline have two daughters, Hayley and Kim. Their ages correspond with Simone and me. Hayley and Simone consequently spent a lot of time together, and Kim and I did likewise. We would see each other on weekends, we would go on holiday together, and sometimes we even saw each other before school when Mum used to take Simone, Hayley, and Kim to school.

I would have to say that friendship does not frame our picture—we were actually a close-knit family. Even though I was young, I could sense that the love and life we shared with the Wilmer's was a well-oiled machine, while most of our relationships with blood relatives were spluttering, clapped-out bangers. If there would have been a race between those metaphors, the Wilmer's would win by a country mile. There was a reoccurring, underlying tension with various members of my family's blood relatives. We shared each other's company and the smiles could be genuine, but underneath it all, we just didn't belong together.

The Wilmer's gave me the gift of nurture. They were a big part of my family environment, and I always felt safe when

I was in their company. When I think of my childhood spent with the Wilmer's, I see a garden savouring the last bit of light on a summer day. The radio is playing music from the late eighties and early nineties. The grass is browning slightly under the strain of a persistent sunshine. As I peer out from behind the bushes, I see Mum and Caroline preparing a salad; I see Dad and Bozey drinking beer and turning meat on the barbeque, and I see four happy children playing in the garden. I can hear the bubble and trickle of Bozey's fish pond, and I can see my family dog, Snowy, a white Labrador, chasing after Chloe, the Wilmer's black Labrador. In that memory I feel *home*.

Friendships can be cycles. After ten years, the Wilmers and my family started to see less of each other than we previously had. The intensity of friendship may have dwindled, but the love we felt for each other was as strong as ever, and if we ever needed each other, it was understood that we would be there without question. That need came for my family when Dad died. On hearing the news of Dad's heart attack, Bozey and Caroline abandoned their weekend away that they were driving towards and headed back to be with us.

In the first year after Dad died, I spent a lot of time at the Wilmer's home. They helped me through many dark days. Being at home reminded me of Dad not being there, and so I went to a place where Dad still had a presence but was slightly removed. Sometimes I have thought that Dad's work colleague took over from Dad as my father figure, but that was never the case. The man who was there for me at every turn for that first year was Bozey. He was my link to Dad, my confidant, a rock for me.

The image that defines the relationship with the Wilmer family is the front row at my dad's funeral. Bozey, Caroline, Hayley, and Kim were on the front row with my family. As the service moved forward like a daunting army that could not be stopped, we each put an arm around the person next to us. If you looked at us from behind you would see a line of people linked together in grief and support. If Dad was watching, I'm sure he would have smiled at this show of togetherness. The Wilmer family and the Maloney family will always be united.

The Wilmers created the blueprint. They helped shape my idea of what a friendship is. It is unconditional acceptance, being there for each other through both the good and bad times. I found this friendship in two other friends, Bradley and James Fairbrass.

I met Bradley and James Fairbrass in reception class at primary school during our first week. They are identical twins, and although it is easier to tell which one is which now, when they were young it was impossible. To reduce the difficulty, their nana knitted them school jumpers with the first initial of their names on them. If the three of us were sat down and told that for over twenty years we would remain friends, I don't think we would have been able to quantify such a time span—twenty years to a child is unthinkable.

Bradley and James's dad, Steve, told me how he watched his sons with pride as they accepted me without question. He watched as we interacted together as equals. The disability was not worth a bat of an eyelid. I can still see the three of us walking to their house from school, me bounding along like a deer that hadn't quite mastered walking yet, flanked by Bradley and James. My disabilities have never been an issue for Bradley and James; they dismissed them like a gentle morning breeze that you pay no mind to. Children are unused bits of clay, and parents can mould their beliefs and shape how they behave. Steve and Jill raised Bradley and James in such a way that their minds were parachutes. Our friendship was able to flow and work because their minds were open. If their minds had not been fully opened, the friendship would have fallen swiftly to the ground, like a parachute that failed.

The quality that has always struck our families, our friends, and all three of us is the determination that we have had to keep our friendship together. Our friendship has survived living in different parts of Peterborough, different school classes, different secondary schools, different cities, and even different countries. The task is much easier these days, as technology has shrunk the world. Now, a friendship can live, breathe, and thrive over text messages, e-mails, and social networking sites. However, these are only tools, and we have had to be productive with our friendship. Someone can have all the tools to complete every DIY task known to man, but if he just keeps them in the garage nothing will ever get done. We have utilised these methods to make sure we keep our friendship fresh, and although when we get together there is a catch-up phase, it is never an awkward 'so, we haven't seen each other for ages, what do we talk about, and where do we start?'

As we got older, I got to know Bradley and James's sister Dani. We saw each other on nights out in Peterborough and had drinks together. I got to know her as an individual rather than just my best friend's sister. Finding a friendship with Dani was a gift, because it felt as if my family bond with Bradley and James had been expanded and enhanced.

By chance, I ran into Dani in Peterborough once. At the time, I was in a very bad relationship, and so Dani and I sat in the Queensgate shopping centre and talked. I don't know how long we spoke—it seemed that time suspended itself. I was going through some really hard times in my life. I felt ugly and inferior to everyone. My personal life was a fallen empire: it was Rome after the Goths sacked it. It was such a refreshing change to talk to someone and not feel my words were being judged. I had lost my way in life, and I didn't know what direction to take. I was keeping the company of people who were hurting me. Talking to Dani on that afternoon reminded me of how I should be treated, which was with respect. I was an equal again.

James and I had a falling out. It was not a massive shouting match, but it was a disagreement that had legs and it ran and ran. The reason is not important, but after the dust settled, it became clear to me that other people involved had exasperated the situation, and our friendship became the victim. I think if I hadn't listened to other people whispering in my ear, it would perhaps have had a better outcome. I was sad and angry at the time but also very proud. James and I both dug our heels in like the stubborn mules we are, and neither of us wanted to give an inch. Then James moved to America. The situation was in a state of deadlock for a number of years. Time thawed the ice and the deadlock is now broken. James is still in America, but I feel so much closer to him now that our issues have been put to bed.

The falling out with James taught me two important lessons regarding friendship. One was that regret is a hard thing to live with. We wasted so much time being angry and not sorting our issues out when we could have enjoyed being friends. It is true that friendship is a terrible thing to waste, and unfortunately James and I have learnt that the hard way. The other lesson was that one should never let a third party hold sway over a friendship one has. The two friends need only talk their differences through between each other rather than letting outside influences load a gun and shoot the friendship in the foot.

A girlfriend once observed that I talk about the Wilmers and the Fairbrasses, who were features of my early childhood, and I talk about the friends I have as a grown-up, but I do not speak about the friends I have had in the intervening years. And that is because there were not really many friends of any note to mention. I roamed around different friendship groups without really finding a place to settle. It is a natural process that as you leave school, some if not most of the friendships you have start to wane a little and fall by the wayside. For me one friendship has remained constant since my days at secondary school.

I met Adam McGeever in September 1993 at Jack Hunt School. He had been reading a Peterborough United programme from the previous season and had spotted my picture. I had been a mascot for a game against Cambridge United, and because Adam was a big Posh fan he wanted to talk to me about it. I suppose this initial exchange laid the foundation for our friendship. It sits happily with me that our friendship has been built on a mutual love of Peterborough United. We have a much broader range of conversation topics now, but if all fails, we can always talk about how the Posh team of the 2001/2002 season failed to get promoted.

Even at the age of eleven, Adam was tall. He had short brown hair that carried the promise or threat of curling if he let it grow. He seemed to be full of year-seven enthusiasm, or maybe that was just because he had found a fellow Posh fan who was so dedicated to the cause that he had been a mascot. He was not in my form or any of my classes at the time, which meant our paths didn't cross that often.

It was not a friendship that was like the biblical story of genesis where our friendship was formed instantly and we became inseparable. My friendship with Adam was more like Darwin's theory of evolution. Our friendship went from a hello on the playground, which would probably be classed as a single cell organism swimming around in the sea, and progressed to being an ape as we spent more time together when we sat together in science lessons. We became cave men by sixth form, when we would have the odd night out together, and finally we graduated to a fully developed man on the Darwin evolution when we developed our friendship after we left school.

I was reaching out for friends who were drifting away after school. I felt a bit as if I was drifting all alone in space. In those circumstances, I may have been unlucky and grabbed hold of a friendship that wasn't going to stand the test of time. However, this wasn't so; without the restrictions of the school environment, my friendship with Adam thrived. When Adam moved to Birmingham it could have had an adverse effect on our friendship, but the distance made it necessary for both of us to make the extra effort to keep in touch. We would talk to each other every time Posh played. If I was at the game, I would send Adam text updates. I was again determined to keep our friendship intact, just as I did with Bradley and James.

Adam never really returned to Peterborough after university. He had a brief stay at Reading University before decamping to France. Initially, these moves got me down, as I was unable to see him as much as I would have liked, but in a way the distance enriched our friendship because when we did see each other it encouraged us to make the most of the experience. That doesn't mean we take part in some adrenaline-fuelled extreme sport, but we do appreciate doing the normal things like going to the pub or having a curry together.

Simone said to me once that she thought Adam and I spoke a different language. I think that is true in a way that we both get each other. One of us will make a comment about something that happened ten years ago and we will belly laugh or we will theatrically use a double negative to describe our actions, such as 'I ain't done nothing wrong!'

We went to a play where we said to one of the actresses afterwards, 'I hope you're not as wooden in bed as you are on the stage!' I know, this sounds very harsh, but we found it funny.

Another time I threw a school-days acquaintance out of my car because he said his tax contributions had funded my motorbility car. These stories may not have made you laugh, which is really my point. It is such a blessing to have a friendship where the same things make you laugh and the other person knows what you are talking about without a need for an explanation.

I have always related Adam's and my friendship to part of the chorus in the song 'Live Forever' by Oasis. 'I think you're the same as me/We see things they'll never see/You and I are gonna live forever.' And that defines our friendship: we get the jokes that no one else gets, and our friendship is so comfortable it will last forever.

Every friend in this chapter has taught me something or brought something to my life. Sandi Frost is the personification of a magic potion. I was dying inside when I met her. My personal life was a cancer that was engulfing my whole body. I was having an identity crisis; I was being ground down by a relationship that was just a vicious punishing circle. We would break up in the morning and get back together in the evening, which was leaving me winded. Just when I had started to tire, Sandi came into my life and her friendship potion breathed new air into my flagging life.

It is hard to be practical where meeting Sandi is concerned. There seems to be too many twists of fate involved for me to be able to discount them all. We met on a counselling course that I wasn't even supposed to be on; I had booked a place on a course at the adult college in Peterborough but at the last minute the course was cancelled and I was left scrambling round trying to find a place on a different course somewhere. I managed to secure myself a spot at Peterborough Regional College and that is where a woman named Sandi sat next to me. Fifteen minutes into the course we were sharing our problems as a part of an exercise. I was expecting the conversation to be awkward but it felt natural from the start. This was the beginning of a beautiful friendship.

For the first few months, we would only see each other once a week in class. Gradually the friendship became more intense, and we would see each other when the class had a night out, and then I would pop around to her house for tea. To most people surrounding me, Sandi and I being friends seemed weird; Sandi was a married woman with children, and she was older than I was. A few people, my girlfriend included, thought that something romantic must have been going on, but that was never the case. I accepted that the friendship that was developing looked strange, but it was and has always been purely platonic. My then-girlfriend stamped her feet and accused me of underhanded skulduggery. She wanted to end Sandi's and my friendship but something inside of me was telling me that I needed this friendship, which led to me being determined not to bow to the demands that were being levelled against me.

My relationship was like a plank of wood that was very weak. It was starting to splinter and crack on a regular basis. If you kept jumping on the plank and applying pressure, it would be only a matter of time before it snapped in two. The relationship kept getting worse and worse until it became like a throbbing pain in my body. Everyone could see the final break coming; I knew it was coming too, but I couldn't make the clean break for myself. I didn't think I could stand the pain. But when the plank of wood finally snapped and my relationship shattered, Sandi was one of the first people to help me back to my feet.

The break-up was painful. It was almost like grief. I had lost the person who had been central to my life, but it led to my friendship with Sandi becoming strong and intense very quickly. I became a constant fixture at her family home, and we were in constant contact. Sandi would text me most days, and I'm not sure if it is healthy to say but she did become my lifeline. I had almost become a recluse during my two-and-a-half-year relationship, and I had forgotten the social, outgoing person I used to be. Sandi encouraged my head to creep out from my insular shell.

Sandi integrated me into her family quickly. I met her husband Jason, one of her brothers Duncan (who it transpired had been in the same sixth form that I had), and her sister Hannah. We went on nights-out to a really run-down pub in town for karaoke, and we went for breakfast together. I watched football with Jason, ate pizza with Hannah and her family, and went to the cinema with Duncan. Some people thought the change of direction in my social life was bizarre and wondered where these people had come from, but it just felt so natural to be around them.

There is no sugar coating with Sandi. She is incredibly honest. She is not a claque who laughs and applauds my actions on command. If I have treated Mum badly by not ringing her after a doctor's appointment, Sandi will tell me. If she disagrees with one of my opinions, she will let it be known. I think that is such a healthy part of our friendship;

the last thing I need is 'yes' friends who just agree with everything I say. Sandi is an empathic person, and what you see is what you get. As a consequence, I have become more congruent with other friends, and I am not afraid to let someone know if he or she has have behaved badly. I am now perfectly willing to have an argument in a public place if it is for something I believe in. It is a great lesson to have been taught.

I started to heal over time, and like a caring person who has picked up a bird with a broken wing and nursed it back to health, Sandi threw me up into the air and let me fly. I added to my friendships I had made with her family by branching off and making new friends with people who Sandi had introduced to me. I became friends with Nicki and John, a couple who have become a regular part of my life. In fact, I must say that apart from being great friends, they also helped me put this book together. Without their help, it would have stayed a disjointed series of rambling chapters.

I am not sure if I believe in a higher power or divine intervention, but it is clear to me that Sandi was brought into my life for a reason. I needed someone to show me what I had to offer the world. Sandi and her family helped me back on the track when I had careered off course. They became a big part of my life and became an extension of my family. I couldn't imagine my life without even one of them in it. I love them all dearly, and each member of the family brings something different into my life.

My involvement with Sandi's family has blossomed. Over time, I also met her other two brothers, Adam and Andrew, and her mum and her dad. There is an ease of laughter that flows through our relationships. Adam and I have a different friendship: it is fun and silly. That is not to take anything away from my other relationships with the family members.

I think we just clicked straight away. Adam and I are very much on the same wavelength—we are a bit like Ant and Dec, just with an eighteen certificate.

Sandi was there when I thought my life had ended, but she was also with me when I went through a rebirth. My life feels so enriched now, and it feels that it was necessary for it to end so that it could start again. Not a week goes by when I don't look back and say, 'If that break-up hadn't have happened, I wouldn't have such a good life with such great people.' Sandi and her family have been a huge part in the redevelopment of my life.

I said to James Fairbrass once that I didn't think that another album would come along that would mean as much to me as Oasis's first two albums. I said that I would hear music that I would like, but I didn't think I'd feel the thrill of hearing an album that spoke to me. I think before I met Sandi and her family, a lot of my friendships had become like that: there were some good songs that I really liked and there were some one-hit wonders, but they didn't touch me. Sandi and all her family came along, and they were the album that I didn't think would come—the album that touched me—and I knew that they'd stay with me forever.

You don't have to be disabled to feel alone in this world. However, at times, a disabled person can feel more alienated than your average person can. There has been rejection in my life of various forms. I think it is very hard to make it through life on your own; I certainly couldn't do it. The four friendships I have described have contained unconditional acceptance on both sides and unconditional love. These people are my pyjama friends. When I am with them I feel so comfortable and accepted. Just like pyjamas, they seem to blend around me. These friends are part of me, and I feel very blessed to have them in my life.

15

THE DEDICATED THINKER OF FASHION AND GROOMING

I refuse to accept that because I am disabled I have to wear elastic waist trousers and baggy T-shirts. I put a lot of thought into what I wear. I try to find ways to overcome or circumvent obstacles and this includes clothing. For example, I do not own a pair of shoes that has laces. I didn't learn how to tie my shoe laces until I was eight, and I tend to avoid them if at all possible. My shoe cupboard consists of slip-on shoes and Velcro trainers. I try to keep it simple without compromising on style. I think I have been scarred by those hospital-issued boots of my youth!

I encountered two clothing problems when I moved up to secondary school. One problem was that I had to wear a tie, and the other problem was that I had to wear a shirt, which meant I had cuffs to deal with. Mum could put my tie on at home, but when it came to getting dressed after the PE, I was in trouble. The embarrassment of having to ask the teacher if he could help me with my tie forced my hand and I dedicated my time to learning how to tie it myself. In the end, I succeeded by combining the use of my hands with the utilisation of my mouth as a holding device. It wasn't a conventional method, but it worked.

The cuffs were another matter. I never got the hang of them. They are impossible because the process renders one hand redundant, which doubles the difficulty of an already fiddly task. It's actually amazing to think that it took two and a half years to come up with the simplest of solutions: roll up the sleeves. Mum would roll the sleeves up after ironing and that painted over the cracks the problem caused. I started a mini trend once in year ten when my science class table, led by Adam, rolled up their sleeves. It only lasted for about half a day, but still, not many people can lay claim to starting any sort of fashion frenzy at school. Around 2006, it came to my attention that roll-up sleeves were in fashion. It was cause for celebration, and my wardrobe was quickly peppered with a number of said items. Even if this style goes out of fashion, I vow that it will never go out of my wardrobe.

Damn the jeans industry! Somewhere along the line in the last decade, some bright spark decided that button-fly was the way to go with jeans, and like lemmings, everyone followed. But did they show any consideration for disabled people who needed zip-fly jeans? No, they did not! They forced us to either adapt or scratch around at the bottom of the jean pool looking for scraps of denim that still harboured zip-fly! I tried button-fly, I really did, but after I spent an hour in a toilet stall one evening trying to do the buttons up, I called time on the experiment. However, there has been a saving grace for me. Over a period of years, I have forged a strong link with a clothes shop in town called Clues. Early on, I explained my jeans predicament to them, and they have always been understanding and helpful. When I go jeans shopping, they are kind enough to go through their stock to see if they have any zip-fly. It has even got to the point that if the boss is out purchasing new stock, and he sees a pair of jeans with zip-fly, he will buy them. He knows he's on a winner, because I will snap up any quality zip-fly jeans as they are quite rare.

For reasons that only he can explain, Adam loves France so much that he lives there. He came back for his twenty-sixth birthday, and I picked him up from the airport. On the ride back to Peterborough, we discussed the plans for his birthday party. We were going to have a meal and then a few drinks with dancing optional afterwards. Knowing Adam's food tastes, I was spot on with my diagnosis when I said, 'So, when you say a meal, you mean a curry, right?' The answer, of course, was 'Yes', and to which I responded, 'I had better wear black then!' I went out the next day and bought a new black shirt from Clues, roll-up sleeves of course! This is another thought-out fashion move: if I know I am going for a meal that may cause spillages on my clothing garments, I avoid the colour white. I know from experience that the messier the meal, the more chance there is of me spilling something down my top. To lessen the impact of such events, I wear dark colours as my chosen armour. Ironically, by wearing a dark shirt to a messy meal, I am far more relaxed about a potential spillage, and I end up not incurring the wrath of messy food.

Time and time again, my life with disability has been all about adaptation, and that's what I do with the clothes I wear. Some might say I'm a dedicated follower of fashion, but I prefer to look upon myself as a dedicated thinker of fashion! But clothes are just part of the 'look' for anybody. There is no point in wearing great clothes if the rest of you looks like a dog's dinner! I had a shaved head for large chunks of my childhood until I ventured into the realms of hairstyles.

My double crown didn't help matters, and sometimes I struggled to get my hair just right, which was annoying. But in my twenties, fashion's wheel of fortune smiled on me when it deemed the messy haircut to be 'in'! The real bone of contention for me however, was shaving.

I didn't quite know how to hold a razor. The holding of the instrument sounds quite inconsequential and insignificant until you consider the pitfalls of shaving with earthquake-shaking hands. One poorly controlled movement and blood will not hesitate to stage a mass emigration away from my body. The first time I touched my face with a razor I nearly cut off my nose, and with my second stroke, I nearly cut off my mouth. The pain shot through me and blood spurted. The blood ran into my mouth and added to my feeling of bitterness; I asked, 'Why is everything so hard?' The water in the sink went from clear to red, and the shaving foam became a shade of pink. For practical reasons, Dad took over shaving me after those near-defacing incidents. This plan was flawed; I wasn't learning how to shave, only how and when to tilt my head for Dad to shave me. When Dad died, the chickens came home to roost.

Our family friend, Bozey, brave man, stepped up to the plate. He taught me how to shave, which should have been Dad's and my plan. It was a hard and scary experience for Bozey; I always joke that he had a full head of dark hair with no grey in it before he taught me how to shave. He now has no hair, apart from some grey stubble.

Bozey taught me everything I needed to know to shave, but he could only do so much. It must have been hard for him, looking on, as I would cut lumps out of my face at regular intervals. I would go round his house three times a week and stand in front of the mirror; my nerves would be bubbling up within me as if boiled in a kettle. I knew it was only a matter of time before I cut myself. I would then have to wade through puddles of blood until the shave was finished.

The healing power of the human body amazes me. I could have filled a blood bank lab with the results of my shaving injuries from 1999 through mid-2000. I am absolutely dumbfounded when I look at my face and see no scars from my early razor encounters.

I bought a new white shirt for a night out once. I showered and then disaster struck! I cut my chin so badly that I thought it was going to fall off. There was blood in the sink, blood on the floor, blood on the mirror—even blood on the walls. I felt so embarrassed. I looked as if I had been shaved by Sweeney Todd and was heading for one of Mrs. Lovett's pies!

I vowed not to be defeated, thus despite my chin looking as if I had caught it in a butcher's meat cutter, I donned the white shirt. I got to the pub and people were asking if I had been attacked. It became very clear that the cut was not going to stop anytime soon. I don't know whether I should be proud of my utter pigheadedness or dismiss my actions as complete folly. Although I looked like attractive prey for a thirsty vampire, I do give myself credit for not cancelling the night out and hiding away while my chin shed bucketloads of blood. But, for the life of me, I don't know why I insisted on wearing the white shirt. By the end of the night, it looked like a doctor's operating gown after a ten-hour procedure!

Shaving has been very much a trial-and-error process for me. After all the cuts, all the blood, and all the times looking like a bloody mess, I learnt how to shave. I wouldn't have made it without Bozey's teachings. Learning to shave sounds like such a small accomplishment, but it is without a doubt one of my proudest achievements. I am very thankful to Bozey for making such a telling contribution to my life. I can't believe that I actually enjoy shaving now—well, as much as can be expected. I think it's because shaving was such a monumental obstacle for me to overcome that I feel so proud. It's hard shaving with a permanent shake, but I love the feeling of being freshly shaven.

From the first venture into slicing and dicing where I chopped off half my face in two strokes, I have learnt, developed, and moulded a shaving technique that works for me. I started off using one hand to shave, but over time I have taken to using both hands to hold the razor while I make big strokes. One hand holds the razor while the other rests on the top of the holding hand a bit, like how a person would hold the butt of a handgun to keep it steady. It does seem like a flawed plan—surely two shaky hands are indeed worse than one—but that is not the case. Maybe it is that two negatives make a positive, combining to steady the ship and providing me with enough poise to put together a gliding motion. I rarely shave on an empty stomach as a low blood sugar level leads to more shaking and therefore an increased risk of a higher blood loss.

One of my tricks to shaving is to only use the blades two times before I throw them away. Most people think this is excessive, but having the blades sharp and new seems to give me a better shave, and I cut myself less. I came up with a little two-line poem that amused me to explain the 'two shaves and throw away' principle.

'Keep them fresh
Keep your flesh!'

16

CHARLES

On the day my dad died on the fourteenth green of Middleton Hall Golf Course, Charles was a hole behind. Charles was a member of the rescue party who tried to get the ambulance to Dad as fast as possible. In order for the ambulance to see where Dad was, Charles stood on a hill and waved the fourteenth's flag in the air. Charles was a funeral director at that time, and he organised Dad's funeral. Charles and Mum worked together to put Dad's memorial plaque in place. Charles had just split up with his wife, and Mum and Charles became close; I suppose it was like two lost people finding each other. Mum and Charles were married in 2004. You couldn't make that up.

The last paragraph has just put so much in perspective. I made my peace with Charles being part of our family a long time ago, but it wasn't until I wrote about what Charles tried to do for Dad that I see I should have thanked him. It's the greatest irony of all that Charles was trying to save my dad, but I acted as if he had stolen Dad's place. Writing it down has given me clarity, but a seventeen-year-old sees things very differently.

My first impression of Charles was as a funeral director—nothing more, nothing less. He was dressed in an immaculate dark suit. His shoes sparkled like a clear stream being hit by bright sunshine in summer. His manner was professional and empathic. He had obviously helped many families through the dark aftermath of a death, but his demeanour and responses did not feel robotic. He handled every question, every detail, and every aspect of the arrangements with kid gloves. If our association had ended at Dad's wake and we had gone our separate ways, I daresay we would have forgotten about each other. If our paths had crossed in the future, we might have struggled to recall each other's names and exchanged a few pleasantries before an awkward silence descended on the conversation. I would probably then have said to Mum or Simone, 'I saw that nice funeral director who organised Dad's funeral.'

My second impression of Charles was far more hostile. He re-entered our lives as Mum's first foray into the dating world after Dad passed away. He came to a barbeque with Mum at Caroline and Bozey's. I had been aware that Mum and Charles had seen a bit of each other, but I had not really cottoned on to what was developing between them. I sat in Bozey and Caroline's garden, my mind going through the realization process until my brain sounded the alarm and a red light started to flash in my head. I regarded Charles and saw him as an intruder in my territory. I didn't know what he was doing there or what niche he was carving out for himself, but his perceived trespassing made me nervous and uncomfortable.

Charles started seeing Mum six months after Dad died. I was seventeen, and I was angry about it. I knew Mum deserved to be happy and that she was still young, but I just couldn't come to terms with her being happy with anyone other than Dad. I gave them both a hard time, and I pretty much made it clear that Charles wasn't welcome in our house. I am not proud of that, but I was only seventeen and I was literally grief personified.

Charles had difficulty comprehending my disability. He couldn't understand my speech, didn't understand why I couldn't do things, and generally was at a loss with the idea. Early on in Mum and Charles's courtship, I went with them to Nottingham on a shopping trip. We took a break for lunch where we chatted between ourselves. However, every time I would say something to Charles he would say 'Pardon?' or 'Sorry?' Charles was having trouble understanding what I was saying and a monstrous ball of rage armed with contempt boiled inside me. Charles was frustrating me because I felt he wasn't paying enough attention to me to understand my speech rather than him just not being able to decipher what I was saying. However, as I got to know him better, I realised he has trouble with his attention span where anything is concerned. Charles's brain can be distracted and lead up three or four different avenues of conversation in as many minutes. I didn't have this information at the time, and what I perceived as his reluctance to take the time to listen to what I was saying caused tension in our relationship.

I also did not take into consideration that not only did Charles have very little experience in being around teenagers, he also had very little comprehension of raising someone with a disability. He did not understand why Mum would worry if she hadn't heard from me all day, or why Mum had to know whether I'd had my tablets. His inability to understand my condition gave me a reason to distance myself from him. Exploiting Charles's lack of knowledge about cerebral palsy allowed me to justify not getting close to him. It's another irony that it wasn't until I let Charles into my life that he started to understand a bit more about the disability.

To love Charles as family, we have both had to make steps towards each other. Sometimes he has been like wisdom teeth coming through which the dentist has decided not to remove: they are painful and you can bite the side of your mouth and tongue while you are getting used to them, but slowly you adapt to them being there.

The road to understanding between us has been rocky, and it still throws up the occasional pothole. Hard work and putting in the effort to spend time together, such as going to football, has been a big factor in making Charles's and my relationship work. I think the key has been acceptance. He accepts my disability and all that comes with it. Charles had to get used to my disability. He had to get used to my slurred speech. He had to get used to me needing things done for me from time to time. He now has a greater understanding about why Mum worries about me. For my part, I have had to accept the flaws that I described earlier. He never planned to have children, and so Simone and I were a shock to the system. He has become better as a father figure as time has gone by. In the early years of our relationship, I used to hate giving him a Father's Day card, which was ironic because for the first seventeen years of my life, Father's Day never really registered as an important day. I can't recall a great deal of fuss being made over it in our family. Dad didn't seem to be bothered by the day. Card shops used to taunt me on Father's Day as the word *Dad* would fly out and hit me in the face.

These 'card anxiety attacks' seemed to subside over the years, and Dad and Charles seemed to separate. Father's Day disassociated itself from Dad to a certain extent and allowed me to live in the present by spending some time with Charles. Charles has never looked to replace Dad, thus my participation in Father's Day is neither an act of betrayal or nor trading in the old for the new. The day is uncomplicated—a day to spend with my stepfather.

Charles is a good man; he is not without his flaws, just like everyone. He is frustrating because his mind seems to be a jumble sale where bits and bobs are thrown everywhere and nothing seems to match. His brain is such a confusing place. There will always be oddities about Charles, such as switching off in mid-conversation or not understanding something until you have tried six different types of explanation. I have to remember to relax a lot where Charles is concerned, and when he switches off I have to shrug my shoulders and say, 'That is Charles.'

Charles is far from linear, and early on in our relationship I held that against him. I always saw my dad as such a logical thinker; to a child, he seemed to have it all worked out. When Dad thought about my future, he didn't just think about the next day or the next month, he contemplated what plans needed to be made for the years ahead. For the most part, Charles does not come across in that way, which was a complete shock to the system. Charles and Dad appeared to me to be as comparable as black and white. I didn't like the change in the type of man Mum had in her life, and I didn't want him anywhere near me. However, now I think the differences between Dad and Charles are very beneficial. There is almost a sense of honouring Dad by Charles being so different. By Mum choosing someone like Charles rather than a carbon copy of Dad, she is casting Dad as an individual rather than a mould that everyone else is based on. In a sense, it is a bit like a heavy metal singer changing style and becoming a crooner. Mum executed a complete 180-degree spin.

A while ago, I was worried that I was more like Charles than like Dad. I felt that I had betrayed Dad in some way, because I look after my appearance in the same way that Charles does. I dress well and use moisturiser, whereas Dad would wear what was put out in front of him without much complaining and wash his face with just soap. I worried that I was diluting my father's memory by being like Charles. But I saw that when people are so entrenched in your life, you will pick up certain traits from them. That is not a bad thing, just the effect of spending time together. On the other side though, when spending time with certain people, you will also identify certain aspects of them that you don't agree with.

I have the same beliefs and traits as some of my friends, but that does not mean I am betraying my father. I am like my dad in so many ways, but there came a point when I had to stop modelling every decision, every action, and every belief on him and become my own person. I have met many people in my life and a lot of them have influenced the person I have become. Some people, like Mum, Dad, and Charles, have influenced me more than others. With this school of thought, I see that no one makes you who you are; people can shape you and guide you, but the truth is that you decide who you are. I feel no guilt for having some of Charles's qualities, and I don't feel I betray either him or Dad by choosing not to be like them in some respects.

I love Charles. I think our relationship works. It's taken a long time and a lot of persistence, but we got there together. He came into our life with a touch of a glossy magazine story about him: 'Undertaker Arranges Funeral and then Gets Cozy with Widow', and bearing that in mind, no wonder it came as a shock. He still frustrates the hell out of me, but I know he is there to love Mum, not to replace Dad. I never told Charles this, but I am very grateful for all he did to try to save Dad's life.

17

Hell Plates and Beyond

Driving did not come naturally to me. Doctors had told me years before that because of the epilepsy I would not be able to drive a car. Then, when it was determined that I only had to be 'fit free' for a year to drive, my GP told me that he wasn't in favour of me learning to drive because I would be a danger to myself and others on the road. He thought that the Driver Vehicle Licensing Agency (DVLA) would share the same view. But just as hope seemed to have skipped town, I was given a reprieve, and the GP had to make a legal U-turn. The DVLA stated that I would have to have an assessment to see what adaptations to the car I would need to enable me to drive, but that aside, 'Yes!' I would be allowed to learn to drive. Despite this revelation, my mum was still not keen. It was not because she had a lack of faith in me, it was that she was worried by the foreboding words of the doctor.

Still, I was intent on learning how to drive. I saw my disability as something akin to the threat of a terrorist attack. Countries of the world face up to the chance that a terrorist plot may be carried out on any given day, and the people in those places have two choices. Do they stay at home governed by fear and paranoia, insulated in a safe environment where nothing can harm them? Or do they, as a population, step outside and live their lives to the fullest in an act of defiance, proudly stating that the terrorist will not 'scare me out of my life'? Mum was scared, and to be honest so was I, but I was not going to let fear steer me away from the steering wheel of a car.

The adaptions that had been the DVLA's olive branch and saved my driving dream transformed into double-edged swords. The specifics of the adaptions were both magnificent and mystifying. On entering the car for the first time, my instructor said, 'Lift your leg up.' I did so as I sat in the passenger seat, and upon observing the speed or lack of speed of my legs, the instructor said in a deadpan voice: 'Right, hand controls it is.'

Everyone grows up knowing that driving involves using your hands to steer and change gears whilst using your feet to control the speed of the car. I wasn't going to be driving that way. On the grounds of his leg test, I was sent down the weird route of using hand controls. This involved a ball positioned on the wheel for me to grip and steer with—no ten and two hand positions for me. I would also be controlling the speed of the car via a lever on my right hand side. To accelerate, I pulled the lever up, and to brake, I pushed it down. The lever had a switch that was my indicator. The driving equipment I was using reminded me of the controls used in a plane or a spaceship, and although this was rather novel, I was completely unprepared for learning to drive like this. My whole perception of driving was shot to pieces. It took a while for me to regroup. There is proverb: 'Be careful what you wish for!' After I was confronted with the task of learning how to drive using hand controls, I could definitely empathize.

While I was struggling to adapt to this foreign way of driving, I endured a few hair-raising experiences. Once I took an exit off a roundabout, meaning to smoothly make my way into a quiet part of town, but I lost control of the car and veered on to the other side of the road. If that wasn't bad enough, it just so happened that I had put myself on a collision course with a funeral procession, and I was heading straight for the hearse! Just what you need on your funeral day—to die again! They would have needed a few extra holes in the ground for the driver and passengers in the hearse. Still, at least the person already in the coffin would have had some company on his trip to the unknown.

I didn't pass my first driving test. I was ready—I was driving well enough to pass—but my examiner was very unnerving. She had the reputation of being cold, unkind, and unforgiving in the test environment. When you asked people why they hadn't passed their test, a common answer was that they were unlucky enough to have this woman as their examiner. She put me on edge right away. On the first roundabout, I cut a car up, and she failed me there and then. She allowed no time for the fabled settling-your-nerves period.

I should have turned around, but I thought I might as well carry on, if only to get some test experience. After a number of near misses, such as nearly knocking some children over and running at least one red light, I was told what I already knew. I had failed. My one solace was when I arrived to do my second test: I saw that the soul-destroying examiner from my first test had one of her arms in plaster. In such glorious moments, you can believe that there is such a thing as karma in this world.

My second test was so much better. I had a nice examiner who put me at ease, and I breezed through the test. It was one of the proudest moments of my life. I now had the keys to the door of independence, and I was out of it and into my new car.

I love driving. I love the freedom it gives me. I have had odd periods in my life as a driver when my car has been involved in a crash and I have been without it for a while. Going back to relying on others for lifts really gets to me. Without my own car, I feel my independence and individuality have been confiscated.

Learning how to suck through a straw was my biggest achievement in my dad's eyes, but learning how to drive is definitely my biggest achievement as an adult. There were several motivating factors in passing my driving test. I was again proving a doctor wrong, almost as if I didn't want to change a habit of a lifetime.

I didn't want to be beaten by driving, even though at times I thought that it was a challenge that was beyond me. Driving seemed too complex, too dangerous, and too difficult. The hand controls were hard to grapple with both physically and mentally. I had to learn how to be more refined in my hand movements, and when you have problems with fine motor skills this is no easy task. It was like using a digger to pick a small flower from a flowerbed. At times, my driving instructor would get frustrated with my lack of progress, and I would think to myself, *Yeah, join the club, mate!*

There was no moment when everything came together. Instead, the only cure for my stumbling progress was practice. It didn't matter if I'd had a bad lesson, I got back in the driving seat the next day to try again. I had to have a mental resolve to overcome setbacks such as nearly hitting a hearse or failing my first test. The only way I was able to raise myself to the challenge and in the end prevail was that I had decided that I would not be beaten.

As my driving years started a new set of chapters in my life, tales started accumulating like a snowball rolling down a mountainside. The car, for me, became a pass to take me on what to me were wonderful adventures that will be stored in my brain like places listed in recent destinations feature of a satnav.

I once gave a good-looking girl a lift home from a party. If I didn't know that she liked me before she got in my car, I knew five minutes into the journey as her hand wandered into my lap. I'm sure you cannot blame me when I say that I decreased the speed in which I was driving at this point.

I pulled up at her house in a time that would have qualified me to be a slow Sunday driver. I said to myself, *This is it; lean in and clinch the deal!* It was a smooth, natural progression. My brain, heart, and soul were already chinking glasses and toasting to a job well done as I was kissing this good-looking girl in my car. I thought to myself, *Now, ease your hands into the equation.*

I did this, but my brain was and basking in the glory of the backslapping with his mates, which led to me forgetting the most important thing about my car, hand controls! Suddenly our kiss was interrupted by a movement of the reversing variety and the sound of rustling leaves! After a second, I processed what was happening; I had not put the handbrake on, and hence when I let go of the hand controls, the car rolled back and made us the new inhabitants of a bush! Unfortunately, this curtailed the romantic encounter.

Five minutes later, I was on my way home alone rather than enjoying the company of this girl in her house. My advice to any budding hand-controls driver making romantic moves in their car is this: please remember to put the handbrake on.

It can be a common trait in young men that we drive our cars at fast speeds. On the parkway, the seventy-mile-an-hour speed limit is sometimes treated as more of a yardstick to surpass rather than a law to adhere to.

I was on my way to pick up my mum and sister one day. I had my music blaring, and I was prompting my speedometer ever higher as I flew along a duel carriageway. The tip had ignored boring sixty miles per hour and had only given a brief nod to eighty before it persisted with its hike up the speed mountain. My speedometer was halted in its progress when a police car appeared on a joining slip road. I slowed down but it was too late. I had been caught with my hand in the cookie jar, and my attempt at returning to the legal speed limit was like a child hiding his ill-gotten cookie behind his back when confronted by a parent. When I left the duel carriageway, blue lights appeared in my rearview mirror and the sound of sirens pierced my ears.

The police signalled for me to pull over as soon as I entered a quiet part of suburbia. I was panic-stricken. I had no viable defence that I could possibly use.

The policeman approached my car and I opened my window.

> 'Excuse me, sir, but do you know how fast
> you were going?'
> 'Err, a bit too fast!'
> 'Try ninety miles per hour.'

'I thought it was only eighty.' (As if that
would have made a difference; eighty was
still breaking the speed limit.)
'Where are you going to?'
'My mum's—to take her to an
appointment.'
'Are you late?'
'No.'
'Why were you going so fast?'
'I don't know. I was stupid!'
'Yes, you were! Can I see your licence?'

Here was my only chance to save myself from a speeding
fine; it was a slim chance at best, but I had to go for it. I
started exaggerating my shaking to the point of full-body
convulsions. When I pulled my wallet out my pocket, I
threw it up in the air. I parried the wallet from left hand to
right before gently offering it to the policeman and pitifully
imploring him to assist me. I said, "Can you get my licence
out of my wallet? I'm disabled, and I am shaking too much
to get it for you."

His facial expressions and his stance softened upon hearing
this. He seemed to step back symbolically, and I knew I had
won the battle of wits. After looking round the car, he said:

'I think its best that you do not drive
at ninety anymore, especially when
overtaking police cars!'
'Yes, I won't drive that fast anymore.'
'Now, on your way, and drive carefully.'

I admit it was a blatant exploitation and exaggeration of
my condition. I was facing a driving ban or points on my
licence, so I had to pull out all the stops, and the disabled

card was the only trick I had up my sleeve. It was a saving grace, because if I hadn't have laid on the shakes, I would have become a frustrated pedestrian for sure.

I drove off mightily relieved. I think it was a once-in-a-lifetime get-out-of-a-tight-spot move with regards to speeding. Hey, there aren't many upsides to being disabled, so it has to work in your favour now and again.

18

From 'You've Got to Hide Your Love Away' to 'Supersonic'

A few people have laughed at my disability throughout my life and that has added fuel to the fire of hate that I threw my disability on to. I felt I was an outsider throughout my adolescence, and I so tried to become part of the crowd. I suppose an ironic thing is that my disability allowed me to do so, and in turn, I could camouflage myself. If I am standing in a crowd of able-bodied people, I can blend in with them like a chameleon because I do not look outwardly disabled. There is no wheelchair, no cane, or no leg missing to give me away.

At times, I convinced myself that I had everyone fooled into thinking I was not disabled. I felt I was in touching distance of being human. It does sound strong, but there was a sense of being inferior to every able-bodied person to the point of feeling subhuman. In a way, I tried to ape the behaviour of people who were able-bodied. I wasn't shaking because I was disabled; I was shaking because I was cold. The cover stories were flimsy to say the least, and I was only stifling myself.

I wasted a lot of time hiding my disability from other people, but I now realise I was hiding from myself. I was denying myself time to really get to know me. I was walking around trying to act as if I was just the same as everyone else. What I didn't see was that I would have been the same as everyone else if I wasn't so consumed with being like everyone else. I guess the song that characterized my behaviour would be the Lennon-penned Beatles song 'You've Got to Hide Your Love Away'.

I definitely lived my young adult life feeling like John Lennon's song:
'Everywhere people stare
Each and every day
I can see them laugh at me
And I hear them say
Hey, you've got to hide your love away'

I didn't hear the song until I was a grown-up, but I see my teenage thinking in the lyrics. There is a line in the song that says, 'I can't go on feeling two-foot small', and that seems to define my paranoia about myself. I thought I had a diminished stature because I was disabled, and so if I 'hid my love away', or in my case my disability, I reasoned that my stock as well as my height would rise.

This hiding became less prominent as I got older, but it hung around in the alleyways of my mind. When I met a girl and I liked her, I felt compelled to tidy up the disability or even hide it in the cupboard. As I got older though, the disability seemed to be getting stronger and breaking the bonds that had restricted it for so long; over time it broke out of the cell, looked me dead in the eye, and stamped its feet before saying, 'I want to be free'.

I have had a lot of success concerning my practical dealings with my disability, such as driving and shaving, but the change in my mental attitude towards dealing with my disability was gradual. I slowly found myself being able to tell friends about my disability, and I could even joke about some topics concerning the disability, but the first time everything clicked together was when I was singing a song in my head.

The song was 'Supersonic' by Oasis and two lines attracted me like the world's most powerful magnet:
'I need to be myself
I can't be no one else'

I was twenty-two, and suddenly the penny dropped. I had listened to the song for years just thinking, *What a great tune*, until the day it slapped me on the forehead and said, 'Hey, I'm talking to you!' In that moment, it clarified so much. I interpreted it as meaning that the disability was part of me, so it was time to stop hiding it away from people and embrace it. Out of nowhere, a pen had come down and planted a full stop on my page to signal the end of my awkward adolescence, and I became a grown-up individual.

I stood on the mountaintop naked (metaphorically) for the first time in years, unashamed that I was disabled. In the music world, a lot of people see Oasis as being the biggest band since the Beatles and feel they picked up where the Fab Four left off. For me, in that moment, a Beatles song gave way to an Oasis song. Instead of a song reflecting my melancholy, I was gripped by a song that pumped me full of positivity. To not acknowledge my disability was to not acknowledge myself.

The song 'Supersonic' took on religious connotations for me. I could already have been at the point of throwing away a lot of my disguises, but this couplet gave me a lift to the tip and allowed me to dump all of them in a big waste container. In a moment, the weight of disability had been taken off my shoulders—it was almost as if I was told that it was okay to be me again. Circumstances beyond and within my control had led to a form of purgatory where I had covered myself in misery for the best part of a decade, but finally I was able to move on.

Noel Gallagher wrote the song 'Supersonic', and although it is a great song, most of the lines are complete nonsense that was written in half an hour. With this knowledge, I feel sad, because I know that Dad tried for many years to bring me to the revelation that I had in that 'Supersonic' moment. I sometimes imagine that Dad was in my head on that day and put on the record that finally reached me. He always knew how to explain things to me. My imagination and my rational state of mind are opposed to each other, and the sensible tries to calm the imaginary. I suppose that at the time that couplet pierced my brain, I was finally in the right place to take it in. The seal was broken, and so my dad's reasoning and everything else was able to fly through. At the end of the day, does it really matter how I reached the point where I didn't have to cover up the disability anymore?

I happened to be at work when my realisation came. As I stood in a dank warehouse room surrounded by cleaning supplies, I decided I should live my life according to those lines in 'Supersonic'. I was determined, and every time I hear the song, I get a spiritual vibe that flies over me and it reaffirms my belief in living that way.

Quite simply, being yourself is better than hiding away.

19

HAVE YOU GOT ANYTHING SMALLER?

A person pays for a one-pound hamburger with a ten-pound note. The person behind the counter may accompany the completion of the transaction with the words, 'Sorry about the change', and then hand the customer nine pounds worth of small change. To many, this is seen as a nuisance and rightfully so. Your pocket is now jingling, and you wish that you put your belt on because your trousers are plummeting down your leg as if you were a person dumped in the sea with concrete shoes. The act of being lumbered with an unreasonable amount of change is an everyday irritant that doesn't really register—like missing the bus or having someone beat you to the last sandwich. But for some disabled people, to even use a small piece of change can be a mission that is riddled with difficulty and improbability.

I am one of those disabled people who have to regularly undertake such missions. Using change is a blink-of-the-eye, shrug-of-the-shoulder moment for most people, but for me this daily occurrence is much like walking a tightrope. My concentration again comes into play as my hand becomes a bit like Benny Hill when he would chase girls around in his sketches. The pennies and the pence's are pursued by my cumbersome hands, and in some circumstances the following can happen.

A spotlight seems to spring to life and is fixed firmly on me as I pay for whatever I have in my hand. I am illuminated. I have the feeling or a sense of paranoia that the checkout assistant and everyone else in the queue behind me is staring at me as I struggle to pay for my selected item. Blood sloshes around in my ears and my heart beats faster because I know the terrible truth: I have the exact change needed to make the purchase, thus I feel obligated to use it. I shake and I fumble around in my pocket, searching for the elusive change. I feel like Tom Hanks in *Catch Me If You Can* when Leonardo Di Caprio is always one step away from capture.

I flap my wallet about whilst trying to maintain my cool, but all the while my temperature rises and the shaking gets worse. The wallet seems to be attached to a string and every so often the person on the other end will pull it and the wallet will lurch away out of my grasp. The till assistant's expression can reflect anything from empathy to confusion to bemusement or even disgust. The pained moment is unbearable. We both want the transaction to be over so this awkwardness can disappear.

I open my wallet and extract the money like a fisherman tending to his hooked prey. If I am lucky, I do not drop it all on the counter. But still, that is better than dropping it on the floor, because I then struggle even more to retrieve the currency. Coins are so fiddly and so hard to pick up that at times they feel as if they're glued to the floor. If I drop a one pence coin I deem it expendable and leave it. As I watch the coin roll along the floor, I hear Johnny Depp's character Jack Sparrow in *Pirates of the Caribbean* quoting the Pirate's Code, 'He who falls behind stays behind.' Unfortunately, some people point out that I have dropped the change, and I feel compelled to retrieve the stray sheep of the flock.

If I am blessed, there is no change to be given back to me, but if not, I wobble my way through the process of taking the change from the assistant, and I then get out of the line of fire as quick as possible so my anxiety can subside. I walk away, and the ordeal is over until the next time. My description casts the experience as being like a panic attack, and maybe it is in the slightest sense. My hands go into panic mode as they run around and try to get organised in a similar fashion to when a drill sergeant is coming to inspect the bunks and the soldiers rush around trying to get prepared. For years, I felt as if I would never be fully prepared for the daily ritual of handing over change, so I deployed the use of notes as a means of avoiding the problem with change.

I used notes to cover up the wound of not being able to use change. I paid for everything using money that folded. If the price was sixty-seven pence, I would use a five-pound note ideally, because the change 'over splash' wasn't so great but I was not opposed to using a twenty-pound note to pay for the same priced good if that was the only note I had in my pocket. I could handle notes; they were a low-maintenance girlfriend who didn't demand much time or attention from me. Small change was the high-maintenance girl who demanded my undivided attention every time we were together. If my concentration drifted away from her for one second, she would flounce away. For me it was a no brainer; I was sticking to low-maintenance notes.

The ironic thing about this is that by paying in such a way, I generated lots of change. It was a vicious circle, the more I paid with notes, the more change came into my possession. It got to the point where I had pound coins scattered here and there throughout my home. The money, laying wherever I dropped it, be that in piles or overflowing from change pots, gave my living quarters a look of a place where pirates stored their booty. A friend of mine who uses a wheelchair told me he had a similar problem. He opened his wardrobe one day and found two big plastic bags holding a combined total of seventy pounds. Although my gold-laden lair was not as rich as his swag bags, when you are waking up with pound coins in your ear and one pences between your toes, it forces you to consider other options. Adam McGeever kindly volunteered to take the loose change off my hands, but I graciously declined his offer.

Instead, I had a choice to make. I was a jogger confronted by two different routes. The first one was a flat, easy run where I would not be challenged; I probably wouldn't even break a sweat. The other choice was a route up a steep, rocky mountain. I decided to take the challenging uphill route. When I worked for Mum after my A-levels, I was on a part-time weekly wage. I would be paid on Friday, and by the time Tuesday or Wednesday rolled around, my money had pretty much been spent; all that was left was the odd five-pound note and a heap of change.

I started to set myself a challenge of using nothing but change to pay for things from Wednesday until my next wage packet came on Friday. I then extended the challenge to leaving all notes that I could at home, which meant that I had to deal predominantly in change. I told people about my undertaking of this challenge, and for the most part they just did not get it. The idea seemed to be met with derision and confusion. A few people nodded and smiled, a few more looked at me as if I was more than a tad bit quirky, and once or twice a person would tell me the whole idea was folly. I do think it was something that most able-bodied people did not understand, because picking up a small coin is second nature to them. The challenge started half out of necessity—because I was running out of money by Wednesday—but it turned into an exercise in self-improvement. I knew if I could train myself to handle coins, I would improve life for myself.

By no means was this an easy task to undertake. The use of notes was a habit that I had to kick. I had to make a conscious decision every morning to leave most of my paper cash at home and take my Achilles heel change with me. The task was to stop using a shortcut I had got used to using. I had to get over the panic that infiltrated me when I was paying for things, and the best way to do this was to start off small. My first forays into the pitfalls of using only loose change were made on familiar ground. I would pay for my breakfast in my regular sandwich shop using just the coins running around in my pocket. I would buy a newspaper in the shop next to where I worked. The purpose of this was to build up my confidence using baby steps before I leaped into the rough and tumble world of chain shops such as HMV or Mark & Spencer. I started to be able to handle the pressure better, and although I did not enjoy the small-change exchange, I did take pleasure from the progress I was making.

At times, my cerebral palsy limbs are like computers that have been programmed badly, and they will not move in a way that one would desire or expect. These limbs can be reprogrammed, but the reformatting is a process of repetition. Each time an action that is foreign to my unruly limbs is performed, a single file is rewritten; if the action is repeated enough times then the computer is reprogrammed and can function better than before. After a period of time, this is what happened with my coin-handling skills. By no stretch of the imagination did they improve to an extent which would allow me to dance a coin along my fingers and back again, but nonetheless they improved enough to douse my panic at the time of payment.

I have developed coping strategies that help me in my life, such as using notes to pay for things. Although I have added another string to my bow by learning to use change, one must be practical. The reprogramming only goes so far; paying for a chocolate bar in an empty shop is one thing, but juggling coins over a bar into barpersons hand on a busy Saturday night is a completely different story. I have to assess how the ground lies and when I am in a busy place such as a bar where I may get knocked and drop a coin, the best thing to do is choose to use notes, and then at the end of the night buy a pizza with all the change my note-buying has generated throughout the evening.

Paying for an item in exact change gives me a bit of a thrill. It does sound silly, but there have been points in my life where I have dreaded putting my hand in my pocket to find the correct change. I hate people who crowd me when I am putting my change away and slide passed me so they can be served. I feel insignificant, but I am not; I have untied my fingers and found a way to get by. There is definitely a reoccurring theme in this book about little achievements meaning as much or even more than bigger ones at times, but it is true. I am a sponge and the disability soaks into me. At times, the sponge is heavy, but when I conquer a task, such as handling change, it feels as if a little bit of water has been squeezed out.

Although I do not panic that much when it comes to payment, I still feel a pang of annoyance when I am asked, 'Have you got anything smaller?'

20

CALLING DR HOUSE FOR A CONSULT!

Have you ever watched the television show *House*? Hugh
Laurie plays a genius doctor, Dr House, who solves medical
mysteries that no one else can. His character is partly
based on Sherlock Holmes and it is one of my favourite
programmes. A fellow avid *House* fan once said that I
should write into the show and nominate myself to be one
of the impossible medical mysteries that Dr Gregory House
has to unravel in an episode. That is an interesting and
appealing concept. If the makers of the show ever contacted
me, I would definitely do it—with a walk-on role with Hugh
Laurie and the rest of the crew being my reward, of course.
However, even the great medical maverick Dr House may
have struggled to diagnose the illness that made its entrance
into my life in 2004.

To be fair though, 2004 marked the crescendo of the
symptoms I was experiencing. It was the point where my
body's new enemy stepped out from the shadows and
looked to finish me off. As early as 2000, my new foe was

beginning its first forays into my territory in a series of missions that destabilised my body's governmental system. I started to get huge swellings all over my body, which would be accompanied by a blistering kind of rash. The rash looked like spots filled with pink and whitish poison but they weren't for popping. My joints would be in absolute agony, and I would not be able to move.

We didn't know what this wicked illness was. The cause could not be pinpointed despite trips to the doctors, an allergy specialist, and my chiropractor. The professionals all agreed the revolt going on in my body was a reaction of some kind, but they couldn't agree on what I was reacting to. One diagnosis was a yeast allergy and another was my body finally allowing my grief for Dad's passing to run wild. Mum and I listened to them all. I even lived on nothing but bananas for a week as we went through a process of eliminating foods.

The worst attacks engulfed my whole body, including my face. My eyes would close up and my lips would swell; I looked as if I had gone fifteen rounds with Mike Tyson. I couldn't move my neck from side to side because the rash was also in my throat. My body being ravaged with rashes and swelling made me feel very sorry for myself indeed. I didn't think I could do the whole fight for survival anymore. I was on one knee nursing a bloody nose after Dad died, and then this mystery assailant started to pick on me. My new enemy rushed out and kicked me right in the temple with steel-toecap boots. I landed on my back and looked up; with lethargy running through my bones, I had the notion to just say, 'Fuck this!'

But then, whatever was sticking the boot into me suddenly left. The disappearance was like waking up and realising an abusive spouse had left you or seeing an army withdraw just as they had victory in their grasp. Not that I was complaining! The weird illness maintained the mystery surrounding its identity in a similar way to Jack the Ripper. There was some speculation about what caused such brutal symptoms, but for the main, I counted my lucky stars and got on with my life. However, unlike Jack who slipped away never to return to the streets of London, my mysterious tormentor returned.

Three years later, I was having the social time of my life. I was in Birmingham with Adam McGeever, and we were celebrating the birthday of one of his university housemates, Gareth. It was a glorious weekend, filled with football, nights out, and hilarity. My body, however, was starting to feel the effects of a new assault on my system. I couldn't move without incurring excruciating pain. My hips were bearing the brunt of the pain, as every step I took provoked an internal yelp. On that Saturday, our group of intrepid birthday revellers set off to watch Peterborough United play Brentford. Afterwards, we decided to play knock down ginger in a street full of terraced houses. My choir of pain started to sing as loud as they could inside me, and I was reduced to a hobble rather than a run. I don't know how I wasn't caught by an angry house owner. I think they probably looked out their window and saw a cripple lurching away from the scene of the crime and decided I wasn't worth the hassle.

We returned to Birmingham, and after several nights out I could barely walk. The days would start off fine, but by the evening I was fighting off my enemy with painkillers. On the last night, I got very friendly with a girl called Hannah. Thankfully, she didn't ask me to dance, because I was routed to the spot where we stood. I did see her several weeks after, and we had a far more energetic time back at her place, but that night the only thing I was doing in a bed was crying out in pain. Any move I made, no matter how little, was like an electric shock racing through my body. The only person I kept awake that night was Adam as he listened to me cry out.

The devious enemy of 2000 had returned with a more concentrated approach. This time I wasn't subjected to the hideous rashes, but I experienced severe pain in my joints. Because the attack was so different, I didn't realise that my nemesis was back; I thought that the doctor's prophecy of dying before I was sixteen had arrived on a later flight. I had told several people that I thought I was dying; no one believed me. I suppose it is easy to shrug off when someone is ill and proclaims, 'Oh, I am dying!' If you add to that a belief among some of my friends that I had a flare for the dramatic when I was in my early twenties, then the result was at best indifference. I didn't tell my mum, for reasons that I can't quite put my finger on.

I would lay awake at night and contemplate the possibility that time was running out for me. My emotions were mixed; I imagined an end of two game shows, one where I walked away with all the prizes I could have hoped for and the other where the host said, 'Look what you could have won'. Both scenarios portrayed the positive and negative feelings I had about what I saw as my impending death. I had accomplished so much in my short life, which led me to think, *Well, I've had a good run.* But at the same time, I was twenty-one, and common opinion would suggest that if I were to die, it would be a life cut short. There were so many things I wanted to do, and as I thought about those things, an image came to mind of the game-show host rubbing the contestant's nose in it, saying, 'You can look, but you can't touch'. I thought all that remained was for me to decide how I was going to live out my final days.

I know when my body has a problem. And when I could take no more, I told my mum. We went to the doctor's the next day, and he said that it was his job to convince me I was not dying. I looked at him and my mind mumbled, *Good luck with that!* I took time off work, and I had lots of doctor's appointments, but still there was a big question mark in the room: what was going on? I really could have done with Dr House at this stage to sniff out the problem, but without access to the world of television drama, we were left in a forest with no map or compass and not the foggiest clue of where to go.

I got better and I got worse. The illness was like a repetitive dance song with just two beats. Like one of those infernal techno numbers, it just seemed to go on and on. One day I was on the way out of my GP's office after another round of guess-what-is-causing-the-pain when I mentioned in closing that I had had trouble passing water the previous night. The doctor closed the door and got me to provide a sample of urine. I did and went away not thinking anymore about the test. The next day Mum got a call from my doctor to tell her that the test results showed that one of my kidneys was close to failure.

News like that is quite unbelievable, especially when I already had quite a disability and condition hoard. Everything seemed to happen quite fast. After a few meetings with a kidney consultant, I was in hospital on the renal ward.

The campaign that this mystery ailment had been waging against my body had lasted four years. I had a few victories where I had been able to drive its forces back but my body's territories were fighting not to be overwhelmed. I was in hospital, and I couldn't help but notice how seriously ill everyone was on the ward. People would go home, have a relapse, and be back on the ward in the morning. One couldn't help but take in the surroundings and acknowledge that I too must be very sick to be on such a ward.

At the brink of surrender, the cavalry arrived to starve off annihilation. The doctors diagnosed me with a rare renal disorder, vasculitis of the kidney. Vasculitis is an autoimmune disease where the blood vessels become inflamed and destroy each other. So feeling as if I had an enemy attacking my body was accurate—my body was engaged in a civil war, different parts of me were attacking each other. The blood vessels on one of my kidneys had become inflamed and were leaking protein into my urine. My kidney was leaking protein at the rate of a water skin that is riddled with holes. It was quite a catch for my GP; he picked up on a potential problem through a passing comment and that led the doctors to a diagnosis that Dr House would have been proud of.

The doctors managed to stem the tide and put defences in place that were able to fend off the blood vessel assassination. I found it quite masochistic of my body to inflict pain upon itself but that was just a passing thought at the time. I wasn't out the woods, but with a ton of drugs and a lot of care, my doctors were able to restore some kind of order in my body. The direct conflict between the doctors and the vasculitis lasted two weeks. It felt longer. When the main part of the war ended and the dust settled on the battlefield, it became clear that the drugs would become an occupying force in my body to guard against vasculitis insurgency. The vasculitis had been tied up and put in prison, but its power ran deep and it would always have splinter cells asserting a degree of pressure on the rest of my system. My doctors, drugs, and I had to remain vigilant and guard against rebellion.

I was taking so many drugs that I was better stocked than a pharmacy. I could have sworn that whenever I walked I rattled slightly. In the hospital, I obtained a new record; at my sickest I was actually taking twenty-eight tablets a day! On top of my epilepsy medication, I was taking tablets for blood pressure, steroids, bone strengtheners to guard against side effects that the other drugs might cause, and most bizarre of all, the doctors were giving me a chemotherapy drug to gain control of the kidney.

The chemo drug is used to control kidney vasculitis because it takes the bull by the horns and aggressively combats the problems the kidney is going through. The chemo drug is like a top-class dog trainer: it brings unruly organs to heel quickly. I only took chemo in the drug form, I didn't have to have the radiation treatment, but I still incurred some of the symptoms. I ended up experiencing some hair loss and the doctors said there was a risk of infertility, but it was that or death.

I was on a large steroid dose but unfortunately, they were not the kind that encouraged muscle growth. On the contrary the results of this medication was spotty teenage skin, a moon shaped face and an increased appetite, which in turn led to me gaining a lot of weight. I was not exactly the personification of attractiveness at this point in my life.

I spent the summer recuperating. I wouldn't say it was a miserable process. I laid in every day, I ate pizza, I read books, and I sunbathed in the garden. The hospital kept a close eye on me, and I had to go for regular check-ups. I had to get used to the fact that I would be taking drugs to help my kidney for the rest of my life. Luckily, the chemo was not forever; as soon as my kidney had stabilised to a satisfactory degree, the doctors took me off the drug.

The road to recovery was long. The full recovery took a few years. As the process of reducing my medication continued, all my side effects started to die down, and I started to lose some weight. My hair grew back, and I started to lose the look of a moon-faced over-eater who looked like he was balding.

In a sense, I house all these conditions; we have to live together, but the drugs keep everything under control. I will never be able to pull my drug troops out completely. The vasculitis is a violent psychopath that you wouldn't leave alone with a knife. I completely distrust my vasculitis, and that is what keeps me safe. Since the doctors diagnosed me, I have only had one relapse. The doctors sent in reinforcements and soon quelled the vasculitis uprising.

The solitary relapse aside, I have been able to live with a certain amount of normality. The main discomfort is that I have to go to the toilet more than I used to. It is an irony that the side effects of my epilepsy tablets are that I am always thirsty, and I have a kidney condition which provides me with a bladder that demands instant relief. It is a cruel world! The consultant who oversees my treatment says he is amazed at my recovery, and I have to say so am I. My body was just waiting to have its name called by Mr Death and that would have been it. The comeback that my kidney conjured up is almost as good as Take That's return to the charts.

Sometimes I feel as if I collect disabilities and conditions like other people collect stamps or coins. Vasculitis of the kidney is such a rare condition that there is only one other person in Peterborough who has it. In a pure illustration that it is indeed a small world, Mum works with the daughter of the other man who has vasculitis in the city. I will not be morbid and talk about anything ill happening to him, but if he could see fit to move towns, I would be the only one in the city with this affliction. I would be the one and only: a medical oddity. I think I will challenge him to a disability trump cards game where the loser has to leave town and bestow the title of Mr Vasculitis on the other. I am pretty confident I would win that contest.

The whole medical mystery surrounding my body intrigues me. I guess that is why I poured such ingredients into this chapter. The mysterious foe trying to conquer my body and the references to the programme *House* seemed to compliment the chapter. I do wonder how my body got to be such a puzzle, which leads me to the whim of donating my body to science after I die so that at the very least someone can get some answers.

Would Dr Gregory House have diagnosed me sooner or saved my life in the same time frame? A regular feature of the show is where House leads his team of doctors in what is called a differential diagnosis, which is basically a brainstorming session to find out what is wrong with the patient. These doctors specialise in obscure and rare conditions and regularly one of them will say, 'What about vasculitis?' I feel a bit silly, but every time someone chimes in with the V word I get a bit excited. My brain says 'Ha, we've just been name-checked on TV!' They regularly prescribe my steroid medication, prednisolone, to their patients, and in one episode all three of my disabilities or conditions were mentioned; cerebral palsy, epilepsy, and vasculitis. I'd put my money on the case being solved in forty odd minutes of TV if Dr House and company were involved.

My vasculitis is not a result of the oxygen deprivation that I experienced at birth. It just so happened that it would decide to cling to me like a thread latches on to Velcro. Even though the vasculitis is a separate condition, it is still a big part of my story and another obstacle that I have had to negotiate. Given that, in my mind, the pains I was experiencing were masquerading as ghouls who had been sent as debt collectors to seek payment for me outliving my life expectancy. I guess it is actually part of my cerebral palsy story. Having a disability doesn't mean that that is it and you won't get hit by any other health problem. If and when they come along, they hurt just a bit more because it is another thing you have to deal with; it is another hole you have to plug. When the vasculitis first came on the scene, I didn't think I could meet the challenge, but with the help of doctors, my family, and now only eighteen tablets a day, I was able to survive the onslaught and walk on. I am far removed from the pain of those days, but the sobering thought remains that I could have been dead if I hadn't mentioned a waterworks problem to my GP.

21

SEX AND DATING (OR SHOULD THAT BE THE OTHER WAY AROUND?)

I wasn't happy with my disability when I was younger. Shaking hands, a slightly wonky walk, and slurred speech compounded the usual teenage awkwardness of puberty. As I was a secondary school pupil, I subscribed to the common consensus that what mattered above all were looks and image. I didn't think I was ugly; I just thought that my disability subtracted from my dating marketability. I felt like a nice-looking house that people would think about visiting until they saw the sign *Beware of the Disability*. I was never invited to parties, I hardly went on any dates, and I was never passed a love letter in class. I fell back on my disability as the explanation for this as I couldn't see any other reason that would solve the mystery.

I think there was certainly an element of wariness regarding my disability floating around the female population of my school. Now that I am older, I can use hindsight to extract some minerals of knowledge from the cliff face and gain a different perspective that reads like a quote from a motivational book: 'How can you expect other people to find you attractive when you find yourself unattractive?'

My dad made me feel insecure around women. He said to me once that because of my disability, I would not be a good kisser. I am 100 per cent sure he was joking, but as an insecure boy who had not had his first kiss at that point, I was mortified. I already thought that the disability was a roadblock in my journey towards a dating life. But then my dad, who I thought was an oracle on everything, dropped a bomb on me, saying that once I got a girlfriend I would not be able to kiss her properly because I would have no control over my tongue. It was a throwaway comment, but it did make me very insecure, and in adult life, I would feel the need to bring it up with girlfriends and gauge their responses. There would be an occasional whisper in my ear of 'Stu, your cerebral palsy will make this kiss awful for her.'

At school, some of the kids took delight in asking me questions about what I could 'do' sexually. I knew they were looking for cheap laughs, and I indulged them by answering truthfully. I wanted them to know that there wasn't anything that I couldn't do. I look back and see that these questions were demeaning and really highlighted how dim-witted the boys concerned were. However, maybe they were serious questions that they could not articulate in a proper manner.

Another set of kids gave me quite a prophetic insight into sex and my condition. The conversation was still loaded with humour, but it was positive and actually gave me an ego boost in an area where my ego was non-existent. We were talking in the changing room one day, and one of my friends quipped that with my shaking hands I would satisfy girls very easily. Of course, the descriptive language took on a much coarser form, but the message was the same.

I had never thought of my disability aiding me in the pursuit of the fairer species, so this was an apple-dropping-on-my-head moment. I felt like the first DJ who scratched a record and realised that it sounded good. My friend was obviously joking, but he was right. My shaking hands have been described as magic by more than a few bedfellows down the years, and I think if I was marketed right, I could give the sex toys market a 'shake up'. I do have to thank my friend for making that joke, because I have been passing off his quip as my own for over a decade, and I do not plan to stop now.

Despite the ego boosts from the changing room jokes, I had a distinct lack of self-confidence when it came to dating and sex. I did not quite measure up to the image criteria that so many teenagers are judged by. I felt passed over; there were times when I thought to myself, *They really do not know what they are missing out on*. Maybe I didn't put myself forward enough, or maybe my school years were a sick joke that fate played on me. It was as if fate said that I had to go through those awkward years where I just didn't feel noticed so that when I was older I had the courage to push myself forward more. It is easy to look back at my years at secondary school as character-building, but at the time it felt as if I was going through menopause, and I had faded into the background to such an extent that I was not noticed.

I may have been a little self-critical by chastising myself about not putting myself forward and not going out with girls. I was a young person who was struggling to come to terms with being disabled. My dad's joke had worried me about my abilities to kiss girls, which spread to 'If I can't kiss well, what else will I not be able to do?' There were some cruel barbs being levelled at me by some of my peers at school. And on top of that, I was competing in a market, which despite our protests to the contrary, was superficial and immature. Writing this chapter makes me think it is a wonder I ever had sex. As I look at things as an adult though, I see that everyone feels at the least a bit anxious about sex. Insecurities are not reserved for the disabled community when it comes to sex—everyone has them. They may be physical or psychological, but they are there.

In the years when a lot of young people are going to university and partying or starting their careers and boasting (or lying) about having sex, I was stuck in the slow lane. My friends were off exploring this mythical new sexual realm, or so they told me, and I hadn't figured out who I was. I was suing the NHS, which meant my life was on hold until the conclusion of the case. I was in a state of limbo. As I moved forward, I gained a bit more confidence with girls. Not a lot more, but enough to get me a few dates and a few good times. One such tale was very embarrassing.

In the stereotypical tradition of teenage boys, I had bought condoms from toilet dispensers in the vain hope that I would get to use them. More often than not, they ended up gathering dust in my wallet. They are incredibly annoying things to put on when you're disabled anyway, so fiddly, and when you add in that I shake more when I concentrate, it's a recipe for disaster. I had always avoided buying condoms from shops as a way of eliminating some kind of unexplained embarrassment, which is silly because what is there to be embarrassed about? The first time I did venture into the retail world of condom shopping, I swore it would be my last.

I was working at my mum's cleaning company on a Saturday morning, and later that day I was going to be heading off to a stag party. Up until this point, I hadn't armed myself with the necessary protection. And, of course, on a stag do, you have to be prepared.

The manager of the cleaning company and I decided it would be incredibly funny if I sent a sixty-five year old, toothless, unshaven, taped-up-glasses-wearing cleaner to buy the condoms from Boots while I finished cleaning a Thomas Cooks Travel Agents shop. You've probably already gathered that this cleaner was a bit dishevelled. Please imagine if you will this man rushing around everywhere, arms pumping back and forth. He walked around so fast that he had a quiff at the front where the wind velocity had conspired to push his hair up. We thought he was perfect for the job, and always being one for a joke, the cleaner agreed. Picturing this animated figure bounding in to Boots to purchase condoms seemed like comedic gold.

The plan started off just fine, he went off to Boots while I finished off the cleaning. I then went to the rendezvous point, which was by a clock just outside Boots. I waited for ten or fifteen minutes, but it felt like an hour, and there was still no sign of the condom purchaser. I took a deep breath, knowing what I was going to have to do and took the plunge. I walked into Boots.

I found the cleaner staring bemused at the countless boxes of condoms.

> 'Are you alright?' I said.
> The cleaner scratched his head and said,
> 'I didn't know where they were; I had
> to ask a woman to show me where the
> contraception was!'

> The images of that exchange sent me into
> laughter, and then he said;
> 'And there's so many I didn't know which
> ones you wanted.'
> Still laughing I reached forward whilst
> saying, 'These ones will do!'

But, because I was laughing so much and also shaking a bit more than usual, I fumbled the box and sent the whole shelf of condoms flying. Every condom box was sprawled across the floor at my feet.

The cleaner choose the right course of action: he picked up a box and ran. I, on the other hand, was rooted to the spot, unable to move. I was in complete shock, unable to take in what this latest shaking misdemeanour had caused. I had been transported into a film where the world went about its business at a furious pace but I, the protagonist, stayed still. A sales girl came over to pick the items up, and all my red face could blurt out was, 'The old man's a randy so and so!'

I somehow managed to stumble out of the shop and then proceeded to laugh about the incident uncontrollably with the dishevelled man. I can't help thinking that he had the last laugh on the cleaning manager and I by slipping out of the butt of the jokes noose that we had fitted around his neck, leaving me hanging out to dry as the victim of the prank. After all that, the stag party was an anticlimax. Apart from touching up a stripper, no other action came my way, and the condoms remained unused. It took me a while before I could buy condoms from a shop again, and it was a great deal longer till I could build up the courage to go into Boots again. I would definitely say that that was one of the most embarrassing moments of my life!

I am like most of the population: I enjoy sex. People with disabilities have the same needs and desires as everyone else. At times, people who have a disability are very keen to let you know that they have sex, and they can do so the first time you meet them. Although this announcement of sexual activity can feel awkward, I can understand why it happens. Sex is very important to both sexes, and when a large percentage of society presumes that disabled people cannot have sex, those people feel that they appear even more disabled. Therefore, what happens is that some disabled men and women feel compelled to pin their sexual capabilities to the mast.

I don't believe I have ever been quite so brash as to take my sex life in a sling and fire it at strangers, but when I started having sex I was quite insecure about my disability and how it would affect my performance. I imagined the girls I slept with going back to their friends and saying, 'I had sex with a disabled guy last night; it was weird!' However, everyone has quirks in the bedroom, and anyone can walk away from a sexual experience and say, 'That was strange, they did this . . . 'My insecurities about my disabilities did lead me to overcompensate in the bedroom, sometimes by being very attentive to the girl, and there we have an example of how a negative feeling can turn into something positive. I just needed to relax and realise that sex is relative to the person, and what is deemed enjoyable by someone may not be by another. I had to embrace my 'disability quirks' and utilise my 'magic hands'.

In the way that Kelsey Grammer turned his six-episode part as Frasier in the sitcom *Cheers* into a run of two hundred and one episodes, over time, sex became a recurring character in my life. As I entered my twenties, it felt as if the dam that was holding the dating world back from me started to crack a little bit. I started to become involved romantically with women more often. Although most of these involvements did not lead to relationships, I started to gain a bit more confidence with women. I must say though, it wasn't until I joined Match.com that the dam completely smashed, and my life was flooded with dates, which in turn led to my confidence levels rising.

I have had two stints on Match.com, and in so many ways, stepping into the world of Internet dating was one of the best decisions I've ever made. So much so that I should be the main advertising point in their next publicity campaign. Match.com is an Internet dating site where you 'Make Love Happen'. For me, in my first magical mystery tour of Internet dating, it was slightly more complex than that slogan. Rather than finding love, I found a lot of different things out about myself, and in a lot of respects, I carved out a framework of an identity from being on the site. However, I did cut myself and get a few splinters whilst carving.

I filled out my profile, which if you are unfamiliar with Internet dating is your webpage where you tell potential suitors a little about yourself. I think the previous job field of the person who designed Match.com's profile template must have been in prisoner interrogation because there were so many questions to answer that I began to imagine a bright light beating down on my face and a leather glove hitting me if I didn't give the appropriate response.

Under questioning, I divulged qualities which seemed to appeal to the girls on the site. The dates started to roll in fast; I was more popular than iPod's at Christmas! Match. com started to take over my social calendar. I could barely keep up, and I really would struggle to tell you most of the girl's names that I went on dates with. There was one thing that the profile interrogator did not get out of me though: I didn't mention on my webpage that I had cerebral palsy.

I wasn't trying to mislead the girls I dated; in truth, I rationalised my omission by saying that if I mentioned the cerebral palsy on my profile page, the girls might go on to Google to find out more about the condition, taking a walk down a completely different path to a more severe kind of cerebral palsy. I reasoned that if they saw me in person, the girls would have a better visual understanding of my disability. The theory was sound, but in practice, I could not bring myself to tell the girls that I had cerebral palsy. I must have been a confusing sight for the girls I went on dates with. They must have thought I was drunk, on drugs, had some kind of nervous disorder, had Parkinson's, or was wearing vibrating underwear. It may sound like I painted myself into an awkward corner, but I had some great experiences on my first trip down Match.com lane.

I had never stuck a sign around me saying *To Date* until my adventures on Match.com. In the past, dates just happened unexpectedly, a bit like your average teenage pregnancy. The first girl from Match.com I went out with was neither interesting nor beautiful, but I thought to myself that on the first day of primary school you do not take your A-level exams. I stood at the bar thinking *I have no idea what is going to happen*. It was as if I was a First World War soldier who had just left his trench and was now in no-man's-land, hurtling towards enemy fire and praying that he didn't get shot down immediately. I started to think coming clean about my cerebral palsy would be like dropping an atomic bomb on the date—extreme, I know, but 'first' nerves had been festering all day. It turned out that the girl had a secret of her own.

She was deaf in one ear. I couldn't believe the cheek of it; she had a disability and hadn't told me about it. The girl had exhibited incredibly bad form. Of course I was in no position to judge as that may have provoked a response including stones and a glass house. Strangely, the girl's deafness did not encourage me to open up about my cerebral palsy. I have said that all my dates must have noticed that something was awry due to my visible symptoms, but this girl may have been the exception. She was so self-absorbed that I'm sure she did not notice that my hands were shaking like a dancer's backside in a hip-hop video. She did not ask me one question all night. I felt as if I had communicated to her telepathically that 'I ask the questions!' The night dragged on and on, but she was the one who sent my Match. com snowball rolling downhill, and for that I will always remember her.

I quickly immersed myself in the Match.com environment. A week rarely went by without me going on a few dates. Match.com was becoming a central point of my social life, and I finally felt I was popular with girls. I bounced from one date to the next, taking in everything that the dating world had to offer. I experienced the good, the bad, and sometimes the bizarre.

Once, one of my dates was about to finish when a group of old men started talking to us.

> 'Are you two a couple?' one said.
> 'No, we're not.' I thought this was a
> slightly curt response from the girl.
> 'What's your favourite Beatles song?'
> another asked.
> '"Help"!' I answered.
> 'Oh no, that's not their best song!' the
> third man said.
> 'Well, that's not what you asked. You
> asked what my favourite Beatles song
> was.' This probably wasn't the most

diplomatic way to answer the question, but
I must say I was not taking kindly to these
old men butting in on my date.
'Anyway, what does the lady think is The
Beatles' best song?' said the first old man.
'"Yesterday",' the girl answered after
some serious thought.
'Oh yes, that's their best one!' they all
agreed.
'We're having a quiz this week, if you're
free, we'd like to see you here, love.'

I have since learnt that this encounter is what a man
specialising in picking up women might describe as the
'out-alpha' move. This is a process whereby I, the alpha
male, was removed from the equation so that my rivals, a
group of old men, could chat up the girl I was with. It is hard
being taken to the cleaners in the dating arena by a group of
old men. I didn't see the girl again after that; the date had
turned from something tangible to water that just slipped
through my hands, but maybe she found love with one of
the old men who stole her away from my grasp.

Two people are driving a car. They have kidnapped someone,
and they have put the victim in the boot. A policeman pulls
them over, and upon hearing some noise, the man of the
law asks, 'Did you hear that noise?' The two kidnappers
turn to the policeman and say simultaneously 'Nope!' That
is how the visual oddities that cropped with my cerebral
palsy were treated on dates. The shake in my hands or the
slight slur in my voice probably were noticed, but they were
ignored. It had become such a weight around my neck, but I
just couldn't find the words to turn the murky mystery into
a something that was apparent but not an all-encompassing
definition of me. But then I met a girl online that I really
liked.

I was smitten with the girl. She was older than me and had two children, but that didn't matter to me in the slightest. She had dark hair and was tanned. She was beautiful and made me laugh. For a week, she was the centre of my texting universe. We seemed to get on so well that I couldn't wait to meet her for our date on the Saturday night. She lived in a town that was a little way outside of Peterborough, and I met her there for what I hoped would be an unforgettable evening. And so it proved to be.

I hadn't told the girl about my cerebral palsy, although I really had wanted to; I just didn't want to make it into a big thing and have it hanging over our date like a storm cloud brewing. I have since been told that this was unfair as she had been honest about having kids, but I think that's rather cut and dry. I mean you don't go, 'Oh, you've got kids? What is that?' But when it comes to cerebral palsy, the opposite is true. I suppose I didn't want to cut the buds off before any flowers had bloomed so to speak. On the Saturday night we got into a bar, and I thought that I better take the plunge straight away and tell her what I had yearned to impart all week but hadn't mustered the courage. The words of confession didn't come out easily, much like trying to entice a scared hamster out of its cage.

I tried to tell the girl as gently as possible. I didn't want to dismiss my cerebral palsy, but I wanted to show that I was more than a disability. I thought the girl had taken the news very well, but then she started crying. The tears rolled down her face and every one of them hurt me. I felt guilty because I had caused her this pain, and I could have prevented it. I felt rejection because she seemed to only see my disability, and I felt sadness because what had promised to be such a lovely evening had taken such a turn for the worse.

Have you ever been on a first date where the other person cries because of you, orders a taxi in front of you because they don't want to stay, or ends the date after only fifteen minutes? Well, all of that happened on this date, and I found myself on the way home feeling absolutely shattered. If I had told the girl before the date, things might have turned out completely different, but maybe I had to feel the searing pain of losing this girl so that I could understand that keeping my disability secret did not benefit anyone and could hurt people.

Hiding my disability behind curtains didn't dilute my Match.com experience; if anything it was made stronger. It was my first sustained dating experience, and the amount of dates I had proved to me that I wasn't as unattractive or undateable as I thought. I became a lot more secure because of my first spell on Match.com, but probably the most important thing I learnt was that my disability was part of my identity, and if a girl wasn't attracted to me with the disability or if I couldn't share things about my disability with her, then it would never work. When I returned for my second dalliance on the Match.com site, I was secure enough to add a few sentences explaining my disability. As a result, I became transparent; what the girls saw was what they got. This allowed me to filter out all the girls that did not want to date someone with a disability, and it liberated me. I was free of all the cloak-and-dagger antics that went on the first time I was on the site.

Women really do like honesty. When I put my disability on public display, I thought I would receive less attention, but the opposite was true. I embarked on another set of adventures on Match.com, but with more regularity I was getting second dates with girls, which did not happen a lot of the time when I was hiding the disability. I had casual relationships, I had kisses at the end of dates, and more often than before, I slept with some of the girls. I do attribute the change in the outcomes of my dates to a confidence within myself, because I was happy with my disability. I had kept my disability hidden at certain times in my life as if it was a deformed relative. My first Internet dating experience helped show me that that was no way to live, and it allowed me to put an arm around the disability and step out into the sunshine. Unfortunately, being out in the sun can increase the danger of sunburn.

No one turns up early for an appointment at the Sexual Health Clinic, and no one turns up late. No one wants to be sitting in that waiting room longer than he or she needs to be, because the longer you are there, the greater the chance you have of someone you know spotting you. Of course, you do not want to be late as you may miss your appointment, which would mean that you would have to repeat the sheepish, sideways-glancing walk as you entered the clinic on another day. When you have an appointment for the clinic, you turn up on time.

I was at the clinic just to make sure nothing untoward had come to pass after a night with a girl was marred by the split of a condom. Those rubber rascals seemed to have it in for me. They seemed be intent on putting me in embarrassing situations. I sat in the waiting room, which is without doubt the most awkward and uneasy place I have ever experienced. Nobody wants to make eye contact. It is as if your eyes lock on to another set of eyes, then all the reasons you are both there will spill out. I observed the ritual that everyone else was partaking in and read every poster on the waiting room walls. *Condoms come in many different forms and flavours so find the one that suits you the best. There are often no symptoms of chlamydia.* Once I had exhausted all the posters, I read them all again, just to be sure that I had understood that if I wanted respect I should use a condom.

After the poster proofreading, I craned my head skywards and started to watch the fuzzy television that was showing a news feature on channel four. It was a good way to avert my eyes but bad for my neck. I returned my gaze to the walls where I looked for every crack and blemish. While I was doing this, a girl seemed to manipulate her face into my line of vision. She looked at me in a seductive manner that, coupled with her neck bobbing and weaving to get into my line of view, reminded me of a boa constrictor closing in on her prey. I read an article about how to pick up women in a hospital waiting room once; at the bottom it said, 'Do not try this in the Sexual Health Clinic!' I averted my eyes, as I didn't know what she was 'in for'!

Finally my name was called, and I made haste to follow the nurse through to see the doctor. The doctor was in his mid to late forties. I sat down, and we went through run-of-the-mill questions, and he asked me why I came to the clinic. I answered all of the questions, and then he asked me if my slurred speech was caused by the vasculitus I have in my kidney. Now, I don't expect doctors to know the symptoms for every ailment and condition under the sun, but surely common sense would dictate when you are looking at a form which states that the person in front of you has both cerebral palsy and vasculitis of the kidney, the former was more likely to cause slurred speech than the latter. Obviously not for the doctor I saw.

The doctor was only just warming up as he moved on to my vocation. He read out from the form that I ran my own cleaning business, and he looked up in amazement. He asked if it was right and shook his head in disbelief before adding, 'And you're having sex as well? You do well for yourself don't you?' I was quite taken aback by that attitude; it was almost as if he was a dinosaur who believed disabled people could not possibly work or have sex.

The Bruce Forsyth-like 'Didn't they do well?' comment coming after the slurred-speech gaff really destroyed any confidence I had in this doctor. The only thing left to keep him from being discredited was his use of the right doctor jargon. But of course he carried on his spellbinding form by enquiring, 'When was the last time you had a piss?'

I expect competence, care, and politeness from my doctor, and call me old fashioned, but I took offence to such crude language being used. What in the world was wrong with asking, 'When was the last time you passed water?' The doctor was really not having a good day, had been dared to be as offensive as possible, or was a drunk. Any of those options seemed likely.

After the painful swab test, the doctor called in a nurse to give me a blood test. He told her that I was a 'live one' and that she might have to get someone to hold me still. I interjected that that would not be necessary!

I got the all-clear from the clinic, but what stays with me is the comical conduct of the doctor. Unfortunately, this view is quite common, as is a certain curiosity that surrounds 'disabled sex'. A woman, who was almost as familiar to me as a stranger, asked me if I shook all the way through sex. The same woman, on hearing that I had a girlfriend, responded by saying, 'Good for you!' I wonder if she took classes in condescension or if she was just a natural. I was waiting for her to give me a pat on the head, but thankfully, that was not forthcoming.

Disabled sex might be a taboo for some or it may be that some able-bodied people do not expect my 'kind' of people to be having sex. I would like to go back in time and talk to the insecure disabled teenager that I was. I would tell him not to worry about being unpopular with girls at school, because as he gets older, the female interest will come. I don't think the teenage version of myself would have believed me though. It has been a journey from insecure disabling beginnings to a place where my disability can be embraced as part of me. Now I can proudly proclaim: 'Once you go spac, you never go back!'

22

REGAN

After my first serious relationship of any note finished, I was at my lowest ebb. We were together for two and a half years, albeit we had more breaks in that time than a stuntman with brittle bones. She once broke up with me because I took too long to answer the door. We had something, although I am really not quite sure what that something was other than destructive. In the aftermath of the relationship, I was broken. It was as if I was a corpse that had been through the drainage stage of embalming.

The relationship wasn't always the mirror image of a dead person on a mortuary table. My mum's business cleaned a department store where the girl worked, and this was how we met. We had exchanged pleasantries, but it wasn't until she passed on her name and number to an employee of mine that contact of any note took place. We went out two days later.

I shall call the girl *Regan,* after one of King Lear's daughters in Shakespeare's play for the sake of discretion. Our first date was great, but given that I was not extensively experienced in the dating at the age of twenty-two, I didn't have much to compare and contrast the night against. I made her laugh, and she was playing with her hair. I had the chorus from the Streets song 'Could Well Be In' flowing through my head.

'I saw this thing on ITV the other week
Said, that if she played with her hair, she's probably keen
She's playing with her hair, well regularly,
So I reckon I could well be in.'

And I was. I was so pleased. I felt as if I was on the biggest winning roll ever. It was early 2005, and I had just won the court case. I had financial security, I had just bought my dream house, and I suddenly had a beautiful love interest. I was Robbie Williams when he had the Midas touch and could have literally released a nursery rhyme and it would have gone to number one.

I look back now after being around the dating track quite a few times and tut to myself in response to how naive I was. I thought I was in love with this girl when at very best it was infatuation. My feelings were so new to me, and I fell hook, line, and sinker. Regan knew she held all the power from the start, and I became a junkie fiending for her attention. I needed my next fix, and I would always come back for it. Our first fight was about something so minor that I can't even remember the reason for it, and although we'd only been together for a few weeks, I was beside myself. I couldn't imagine life without this girl.

I put this girl on a pedestal from the beginning. The problem with this arrangement was that I was always looking up trying to please Regan; we were never equal. She had all the control from early on. If she wanted to go to a particular restaurant, we'd go there. When Regan wanted a sash and a fairy wand for her birthday night out, I drove all over town trying to find the desired items.

I am struck by her prophetic words on our first holiday together. We were canoodling in the pool, and she said to me, 'I could treat you like shit and you'd stay with me!' I was angry and hurt at the time Regan said this, but partly because I didn't want to fight in the sun and sub-consciously because she was right, I threw a big black cloth over the danger signs that were going off in my mind and carried on regardless.

Gradually Regan's prophecy came true. I have never known something that I perceived to be so beautiful become something so incredibly ugly. We were a delightfully crafted sculpture that didn't weather well. Every time someone would cast an eye over the piece of art, there would be another crack. Regan would pick a fight if I had bought my sister or my friend a meal. I would then start to lie about paying for the meal, which led to Regan then finding out about said lie. Before we knew it, a miniscule crack led to a part of the sculpture falling off. I was disgusted with myself that I had started to lie because I was not brought up to be dishonest, but it was the only way to keep the peace. I was propping up our relationship with white lies in the hope that it would survive.

I couldn't see it at the time, but my relationship had become a mirror image of British politics in the nineteen eighties. I was Britain and Regan was the Iron Maiden, Margaret Thatcher. To me, the similarities are alarming.

In the eighties, Margaret Thatcher oversaw a country that descended into rioting, record unemployment, privatisation of British industries, dwindling power of the trade unions, and the mining strikes. The youth of the country seemed to accept that the pillows of their lives were being on the dole, daytime television, taking drugs, and bad football at the weekend. Before Regan and I became an item, I was a very social, outgoing person. I laughed a lot and felt at ease in my own skin. I would go out with friends and have a good time. Perhaps more importantly was that I lived in relative harmony with my disabilities. Then Regan came along and the future seemed to offer nothing but good times, much like when Thatcher became the first woman prime minister. However, all the promise seeped away. Margaret Thatcher bled the colour out of Britain. Every house looked like a carbon copy of the one next to it. There was no individualistic flair.

Regan wanted me to conform, to look like everyone else; she wanted me to remove any trace of disability from my appearance. Regan wanted me to work on not holding my drink in a 'disabled way', which is that my elbow rises to being adjacent with my drinking hand to aid my balance and prevent mass spillage. She wanted me to cut out disability mannerisms that highlighted my condition. For instance, Regan wanted me to stop holding my hand by the side of me like a dog would do when it is asked to 'give me your paw.' I would only do this from time to time, but it reminded Regan that I was disabled, and so she demanded that I rid myself of it. It was unreasonable to insist that I tried to banish these disabled oddities; they were symptoms, not habits that I could break, such as not putting the toilet seat down.

Regan had a family who made me feel less than welcome. I felt like the opposition when I was in their house. I would be called 'Shaky' on account of the slight tremor in my hands, which made me feel very uncomfortable. The dad was not in favour of his daughter getting involved with me. What sealed his disapproval was that Regan did an imitation of my walk before we got together. She stood in the middle of their living room grossly exaggerating the way that I walk with a slight limp. She made me look like one of the zombies in Michael Jackson's Thriller video. The whole family had a good laugh at the charade, while the dad threw up his hands, imploring his daughter not to go out with me. I was uncomfortable and hurt when I found out about what could only be described as people having fun at my own expense. I could never trust the family again, but like a worn-down population, I towed the line and went about trying to please my girlfriend.

Thatcher attacked the miners, Regan attacked my disability. Regan would tell me not to hug her because I was shaking too much. I would then try to stop myself shaking, but this only succeeded in making me shake even more. I tried to put my body in an invisible straight jacket, but it simply became more irate and shook even more than before it had been restricted. The situation was brutally ironic because the cerebral palsy, the shaking, and the rest, was not new. The girl had come into the relationship knowing that I was disabled and that it wasn't going to go away. Once she got into a relationship with me, she tried to make my disability disappear, but she only succeeded in making it more noticeable. When I would eat with her, I would sometimes go hungry because I was such a bag of contorted shaking nerves that I couldn't get food from my plate to my mouth. Simple tasks became complicated, because I was trying to follow the given mandate not to shake.

I was a person devoid of any confidence and individuality. My friends and family had been dealt with the same way that Thatcher had dealt with the trade unions. Regan limited the power of my loved ones. I saw less of them, and she dismissed whatever they said. Regan knew that she could not get rid of them fully, but she would not have them influencing me. Cut off from family and friends and lacking any kind of self-esteem, I was easy game for a predator who had stalked her prey until it was at its most vulnerable.

Regan whispered poisonous words into my ear. She said that no one apart from her would ever put up with my disability. She said that if I wasn't with her, I would be alone. I find that when you are in a less-than-healthy state of mind, negative comments are easier to take on board than those that are positive. I stored the words inside me, and they grew like tumours; my soul had been stolen and replaced with something burnt out. She was the head of her own cult—I followed her, and I would do anything for her. I felt ugly and less than human, and I thought no one else would have me. Hence, I had to stay in the cult.

I kept telling myself that things would get better, but towards the end, even I didn't believe it. I was being subjected to a form of domestic abuse. Regan was emotionally abusing me; I was a shell of what I used to be. The insults were mental torture. I could break down at a drop of a hat. I would question everything that I did because I had no confidence. Every decision was made with the view of appeasing Regan and therefore avoiding her wrath. My life revolved around her, and it was a journey of walking upon eggshells. She told me that she was 'less proud of me' because I didn't have a job, but when I started a new business she didn't like that it took my focus away from her. I could not win with her.

In our infancy, every day seemed like a centre-of-the-world moment. As we progressed in our relationship, like most relationships, routine set in, and the centre-of-the-world moments appeared every so often but not every day. I have heard that the love between a couple changes over time, and little things in the relationship become valued as much as the dazzling, world-stopping moments. I subscribe to this theory, but towards the end of Regan's and my relationship, all that was left was the hope that one centre-of-the-world moment might come along to make the hurtful puss that our relationship had become seem worthwhile.

I was no longer alive. I merely existed. No one should be surprised that Regan finished the relationship on her terms. She left, and I should have been happy, but I was a fully paid subscriber of the 'Stuart, no one else will put up with your disability but me' mantra. I didn't want her to go, even though I needed her to so that I could keep my own sanity. It was a case of gangrene, where it was blatantly obvious that the limb was infected and had to be cut off, but the patient could not imagine being without the limb and therefore didn't want to let go of it.

When Regan wouldn't come back and the dust settled, I was left with an empty abuse hole. Regan used to constantly fill the hole in my head with insults, abusive behaviour, and anger. After she left and all the mud-flinging stopped, I was left with the problem of filling in this hole. I filled it by raging against myself. I replaced Regan's attacks on me with my own attacks against myself. If I made a slight mistake, I would castrate myself, citing how able-bodied people wouldn't make the same mistake. If I couldn't do something such as a bit of DIY, I would tell myself how useless I was. It was partly because for over two years I had been subjected to torrents of abuse that I didn't know how to be without it and partly because the girl who I loved had made me believe that I deserved to be subjected to such abuse.

The relationship had an impact on my future. As I moved on, I found it hard to open up to girls because of how I'd been treated by Regan. I had literally let my feelings run through the streets naked in the relationship with Regan, but afterwards I didn't just put on clothes with regards to my feelings, I built walls to make sure I couldn't be hurt by a girl again. I hid disability away from potential suitors in case they had the same views as Regan. There is a legend that after the Roman Empire finally crushed the army of Carthage, they destroyed the city and sowed salt into the soil so that nothing could grow. For a long time after the destructive relationship with Regan ended, I felt as if salt had been sown in my romantic fields. I felt unlovable and unable to trust girls.

Hope springs eternal and I rose from the flames like a phoenix, only this time I had a bit more understanding of myself and what I wanted out of a relationship. I knew that for the sake of my sanity I could never put myself into a relationship that was abusive and destructive again. I went on a lot of dates that proved to me that all the nasty things that Regan had said to me reflected more on her insecurities than they did on my future in the dating market. I reinvigorated my social life by meeting new friends, solidifying friendships, and restoring old ones that I had lost. I realised that I will never let a woman dictate what kind of relationship I have with my family and friends.

I learnt to respect myself and say, 'No, I do not deserve to be treated this way.' That no one—no matter what gender, race, creed, or ability—has to put up with being treated badly.

My feelings towards Regan were very straightforward for a long time: I hated her, plain and simple. My opinion hasn't deviated that much in the ensuing years. She was capable of being very cruel, but she was only eighteen when we first got together, and I was only twenty-two. I don't think we were mature enough to do the whole 'grown-up relationship'. We lived together, bought things together, and made plans together, but we were just children playing dress up. Neither of us quite knew what was required to make a relationship work. The word *commitment* was just a word that was personified by moving in together or a golden ring in the future. Having children was seen as a stamp that would verify us as a family.

I think Regan was very insecure and that much of what she said was a projection of her feelings on to me. She was afraid that no one else apart from me would put up with her, and if I wasn't with her, she would be lonely. Insecurities are no excuse for abusive behaviour though, and even though Regan has made platonic overtures since the break-up, I want no part of it. A person who has survived an attack by a vicious lioness does not keep one for a pet. I won't say I never look back; I do. However, every time I look back, I am so glad that Regan is out of my life.

23

LIVING ON MY OWN

On my dad's eighteenth birthday, he was given a suitcase and money to pay his rent for the first few months, which seems incredibly harsh to me. Mum and I ended our cohabitation when I was twenty years old. The choice presented itself when Mum decided she was going to move in with Charles. This was perfectly reasonable, as they had been together for around three years at the time. I didn't feel rejected by Mum in the slightest. She had a life to move on with, and so did I. The timing seemed to be right for us to wave goodbye to the past and fully embrace the future.

What this meant for me was that I had a number of options. The first one was to move in with Mum and Charles; given that Charles and I did not have the closest of relationship at the time, I dismissed this possible avenue straight away. The second option was for Mum to buy a house for me on the same street she was moving to. We went down this road to the point of closing the deal, but then the sale of our house fell through, which led to a domino effect, and we were back at square one. I then decided that I didn't want to live so close to Mum. This left me with one other route: moving into a council house, and that is what I did.

Flying the nest is seen as exciting: the time that you step out into the world on your own for the first time. I didn't feel that exhilaration, I felt hollow, and all I wanted to do was stay under a duvet and bypass this 'coming-of-age era' that was upon me. The timing was indeed right, but I didn't seem in the mood to embrace the future.

I had a knife and I was chopping my feelings into neat piles of apathy and indifference. I had a few reasons for such tepid emotions about this 'new dawn', but perhaps the biggest piece of indifference that I put in the pile was that the council wanted to place me in a warden-controlled environment. I was disabled and I would be living on my own for the first time, and for those reasons I was classified as a person who was highly vulnerable. The council deemed it necessary for me to live on a sheltered housing complex. I didn't share their view and believed that I was being looked upon as a disability rather than a person. Unfortunately, I had to put up with being pigeon-holed in this instance because the council were not going to change their policy just for me.

Mum and I went to see the place that the council was offering me. The complex looked very quaint—the houses were all bungalows—and it looked a bit like a picturesque piece of suburban America. Unfortunately, this perfect imitation of suburbia seemed to be surrounded by rundown housing estates and unsavoury characters. The complex was an island in a sea of fire.

The house in itself was very small and basic, but you could live there. It had one bedroom, a kitchen, a living room, and a bathroom. I wasn't that keen, but I took it anyway. In hindsight, I should have just turned it down, but in that moment, because I was going to be technically homeless (although I would have stayed at Mum and Charles), I agreed to move in. There were pull cords for me to contact the warden in every room in case of an emergency, and an intercom in the hall to talk to the warden. When people first started to visit, a common phrase that I would say would be, 'No! Don't pull that!' almost as if doing so would mean a trap door would open and they would be lost forever.

Siting on my hand-me-down sofa on the first night in this strange shoebox of a house, the reality of my new living situation began to dawn on me. I knew I only had to pick up a phone and call my family if I needed anything, and in the very worst of circumstances, I could call the warden, but apart from that, I was out on my own. Mum was helping me with the bills because I didn't have much money at the time, but the responsibility to feed myself, to keep the house clean enough to live in, and to take my tablets when I was supposed to, fell squarely on my shoulders.

The first night I spent in my new residence I was woken up by a woman screaming. I peeped out from under the covers, eyes shooting left to right, with my body almost paralysed. A few seconds passed and then a man let out a bellowing cry of 'She's mine!' This was followed by another man shouting, 'No! She's mine!' I am not proud to admit it, but I did go to my window and do a bit of curtain twitching to see what was going on. I went back to bed quite scared. What the hell had I moved into? On the second night, there was a drug bust in the next street up from mine. *Welcome to the neighbourhood,* I thought.

When I moved into the house, I didn't know what kind of help I would need. It was all about trial and error. The first thing I did was to stop the warden from pestering me every day. I suppose everyone has a certain amount of anxiety when it comes to living by himself or herself, even if it is only a worry about how to change a light bulb. Speaking of light bulbs, I could not change them because it is a rather fiddly task; at one point I had to use some emergency lights for a couple of days because I had lights out in a few rooms. I would forget to ask someone to come and change them, and then when I'd get home, I'd realise that it would be another night using a TV to light the room.

Living in my first house was a process of acknowledging that I would need to ask for help with certain tasks like bleeding radiators or changing light bulbs. However, I was headstrong, and I didn't particularly want to learn this part of the syllabus. At times, I would rather put up with a cold house or a loose door than ask for assistance. I saw a call for help as a weakness rather than a quality. I took many years to realise that to identify the need for a hand with certain things around the house, or with anything for that matter, and then ask for help is a quality in itself and not a slight on one's character. After all, everyone needs a leg up at some point.

The area where I didn't mind accepting people's kindness was being fed. My first house was situated on the edge of Peterborough. Adam McGeever pointed out to me a while ago that my bungalow was so far out of town that it was only a few miles away from the county line. If I drove ten minutes down the road, I was greeted with a sign that said 'Welcome to Northamptonshire'. Therefore, not learning to cook at this particular house allowed me to be with other people. Eating at someone else's house had a social element attached to it. I was able to be with people rather than being on my own. I had a reluctance to learn how to cook because I had a lack of faith in myself due to the disability; thus the menu when I did eat at home consisted of takeaway or frozen food.

I have gorged on takeaways for a lot of my life. I blame my addiction on my dad for having cleaning contracts at fast food places, which meant that he would get discount food as well as freebies. I have even blamed my addiction on the Teenage Mutant Ninja Turtles for making eating pizza cool; I swear, if their favourite food was salad, I would have eaten a lot more greenery. Unfortunately, when I moved into my first house, I encountered a problem when I would try to order a takeaway. The area that cradled my slice of suburbia had a dubious reputation, and many takeaway companies refused to venture into the jaws of such a beast. Adam lost his cool once after being refused delivery by several establishments and exclaimed, 'The house is in a sheltered housing complex!'

The quality of the area and the geographical location mixed together with my ongoing court case led to the feeling that the bungalow was some kind of halfway house. It was not my home; it was a place where I was perched until my next move became apparent. All my neighbours were old, and I got the feeling that I was squatting in death's waiting room. Instead of things going bump in the night, I used to imagine the Grim Reaper shouting 'Next!' I was very anxious for the court case to be concluded one way or the other so I could move out before Mr Reaper got his addresses wrong and knocked on my door by mistake.

My ambivalence to my first house could stem from the fact that happiness around this time came in spurts. I wasn't happy with myself, and my social life would operate in cycles. There were times when all I would do was plan my life for the weekend. But there were bouts of loneliness when I would not do anything except sit at home and look at the same four walls. I didn't have many girlfriends at the time. That state of affairs was not what I had hoped for when I moved in. I was under the impression that having my own place would send the girls flocking to my new doorstep. I thought that if I had girlfriends my life would be so much better. If there ever was a flawed philosophy regarding quality of life, there it is in a nutshell. Still, I chased girls and occasionally caught hold of a few, but they were passing ships for me. I was a fun guy who was well liked, but under the social demeanour that I exhibited was a sadness that I was very aware of. Looking back, I should not have assigned blame to the house or my lack of a love life. The reason was buried within me, I just didn't know it.

Despite that analysis, a change of circumstances and scenery brought a new vigour to my life.

Like a disgraced member of the aristocracy, I served my time in exile, and when the court case was settled, I jumped at the chance of escaping the old people's complex and the unlawful chaos of the surrounding area. I moved back to the area that I grew up in. I bought my dream home that I stumbled upon when I was looking for another house in the area.

It was perfect: four bedrooms, a lovely kitchen, an en suite, a bathroom that looked like something from the Roman Empire, a nice garden, an annex, a double garage, and lots more. Each brick had been individually crafted to give the walls a unique twist. There were railings that mounted the wall that stood guard over my front garden, and flanked by two pillars that I like to call turrets, were my electric gates which lead to the driveway.

I fell in love with it straight away. The first thing I was looking for when I started my search for new living quarters was a house with wooden floors. I didn't have a particular love for that particular flooring, although I do like it. My preference had a much more pragmatic strand to it. I didn't want to spill things on a carpeted floor and stain the surface. My previous house had had carpets, and due to my lack of house pride, I had not cared when I dropped whole plates of pasta on it. I wanted to turn over a new leaf now that I was buying a house, and the sensible way to ensure I could do this was to take the hard-surface route. Lady luck was smiling on me when she guided me to my new house, because the whole of the downstairs flooring was either wooden or tiled. I was like a person who looks for beautiful eyes when searching for a mate: if the eyes pass the test, the rest of the package seems to fall into place.

From a practical point of view, the house was completely disability compliant. It was built in 2002, which meant that it had to meet such standards as wider doors, lower kitchen units, and reachable light switches. This was not an immediate concern for me. But it was comforting to know that if my health declined in the future, I would not have to move to a more accommodating environment.

The moment I opened my eyes after spending the first night in my new house, I felt at home. I never felt like that in the bungalow; that place was a stop gap until I got to where I truly wanted to be, which was in a new house bought with money from the settled court case. From that first night to this moment as I sit in my kitchen writing this chapter, my house has always held an extra significance for me. To me, it is more than a house or home, it symbolises something deeper. The house represents the fruits of my family's endeavours with the court case. I fought all the way, and when I walked off the battlefield, I rewarded my efforts with something that will stand the test of time—the house. I have a deep respect for the house, because I hold my triumph over the NHS in such high esteem. I have thought about taking in a lodger, but I worry that not everyone will grasp how I feel about the house. My home is the court case's legacy, and I always want to protect it. I get angry if people treat my house badly, because from my point of view they are disrespecting my accomplishments.

It wasn't until Regan, my ex-girlfriend, left me that I truly felt that I was living independently. I had always had someone looking after me to some degree where my living arrangements were concerned. The help came in the shape of my parents, sister, extended family, friends, or to a lesser extent my ex-girlfriend. For the first time in my life, I was left to fend for myself. Mum was no longer helping me with my bills; I was solely financially responsible for myself, and I was in charge of the house's upkeep. The washing of my clothes was down to me; the choice to have someone iron my clothes was necessary, but the decision was mine to make.

Another area of my life that I now had to take responsibility for, now that I was a resident in the 'Singledom', was catering for myself. In the aftermath of the break-up, Regan's arrogant boast about her being my food lifeline still bounced around my mind's corridors like a crazy rubber ball. 'Without me to cook for you, all you will live on is new potatoes and takeaway!' I don't even like new potatoes, but takeaway food was my rock; takeaway was something to rely on—no matter what kind of food, it never let me down. Nonetheless, for the sake of nurturing both my health and life skills, I decided I needed to get rid of the rubber ball bouncing around in my mind and learn to cook. As if that wasn't enough of a challenge, I decided I would cut down on takeaway as well. On the issue of making use of the rooms I had in my home, I decided I really did not want to let my wonderfully equipped and visually appealing kitchen to go to waste, which meant that I had to learn how to use it.

Adaption, adaption, adaption! This seems to be the key word that defines my everyday functionality. It would really be folly for me to jump into working in my kitchen without taking all possible steps to stack the odds in my favour so that I did not hurt myself. A gladiator can lose his life in the arena if he doesn't know what he's doing; disabled people can lose a finger or be maimed if they don't know what they are doing in the kitchen! Takeaway had protected me from the harshness of this cruel environment, but it was now a brave new world that I was entering. To combat the cruel elements in the kitchen, I had to find ways around the problems.

In order to keep all my fingers—I still have them at the time of this writing—I started to buy ready-sliced chicken or beef from the supermarket, which eliminated the risk of cutting myself during food preparation. I would then put the chicken or beef in a Chinese wok, add a cooking sauce, and make a stir-fry. I explored this method of cooking more, and I was able to add frozen sliced peppers to my food arsenal. My cooking skills were far from gourmet, but they were being built around my capabilities. I enlisted the help of my microwave in order to add rice to my stir-fry meal. I was climbing the ladder of confidence and feeling better in myself both physically and mentally. My friends and family would be subjected to absolutely mundane stories about what I was now cooking and how I was doing it. These stories were anything but mundane for me though. For me, I was Alexander the Great conquering the world.

A month or so into my cooking voyage I was feeling confidence in the kitchen stack up inside me. That is when I burnt myself whilst cooking on the hob. I poured my slices of chicken into the wok that had piping hot, spiting cooking oil in it, and as the pieces hit the pan three splashes of the dangerous liquid landed on my arm. Oh, it was painful, and I bear the scars on the inside of my right forearm, but I learned a lesson. From then on, I always warmed the oil up and then took it off the hob for a minute or so before adding my ingredients. There is nothing wrong with making mistakes if you learn from them, and every time I look at my arm I am reminded of that lesson.

Slowly I was learning to cook. I steamed vegetables, made casseroles, and I was becoming a dab hand at chicken stir-fry.

My cooking artillery was strengthened with the additions of a slow cooker and a steamer. I was able to add to my five a day by safely steaming vegetables. I could prepare a casserole in the morning, eat it at night, and if there was any left over I could finish it off the next day. These aids did give me a hand with safe cooking, and they expanded my home catering horizons a lot. A few isolated people have said that what I rustle up in the kitchen is not 'real cooking', and maybe they are right, but what I learned to do in the kitchen and what I continue to do is find ways to cope that are not restricted to readymade meals. I may not be a chef, but I am a person who has used my kitchen to help myself along to independent living.

In the years between moving into my first house and conquering my kitchen, I have changed dramatically. I am now very independent compared to my early tentative steps into the outside world. I still need some help with a number of tasks around the house, but I am now not afraid to seek that assistance. I have a regular handyman who helps with tasks like gardening or decorating. Having a person whom I can call up and ask to cut the grass or fix a cupboard does not make me a lesser man nor does asking family members make me less independent. It is recognized that I need a support network in place to manage my life. I am living a life that no one expected me to. The odds of me living into my twenties were very long, let alone me living in my own house. Sometimes I can get caught up with the stresses of running a household and curse myself for getting something wrong, but in those circumstances I should really just bear in mind what an improbable life I have made for myself. In the grand scheme of things, is it really such a slight on my ability to run a house in a grown-up way if I can't find a household bill? No, it is not, and every time my electric gates open and I pull on to my drive, I think how lucky I am to live independently in such a wonderful house.

24

TOP THREE ONE-LINE REACTIONS
TO MY DISABILITY

The saying goes 'For every action there is a reaction!' Here's a new one for you: 'For every initial interaction there is a reaction!' I apply this when people first come into contact with me or are first told about my disability and I see how they react to it. Some people take it so well that it's literally as if they've been told I have a splinter. Other people really want to hear everything about the disability. There are also people who feel uncomfortable and don't want to talk about it. However, sometimes people's reactions are more original and provide high levels of amusement. In this chapter, I have compiled the top three reactions to my disability and they follow in reverse order.

Number three:
I pulled up in a car park once, and like I always do, I parked in a disabled bay—and as always, I provoked the *he's not disabled* looks. Sometimes people come up and confront me

about parking wrongfully in a disabled bay. Disabled badge holders are some of the worst offenders; one little old lady punched my driver-side window in frustration when she saw I had displayed a disabled badge. But in this instance, the busybody responded to being informed that I was disabled by saying, 'Oh, good for you!'

I smiled a perplexed smile while I tried to figure out quite what she meant. Did she mean it was 'good' for me to be disabled? If she meant that, she should really have it explained to her that it is never actually good to be disabled, skipping the queues at theme parks aside! Or did this woman mean that I did really well to not look like a stereotypical spanner? I think the woman had flung herself into the murky waters of getting involved in something that wasn't her concern and to my amusement she was drowning. The interaction died at that point because where can a conversation go after such a blunder?

Number two:
There is a man who had legendary status in and around Peterborough. He is the true embodiment of Peterborough United Football Club. Many people have their own special story about what happened when they came across this legend.

I have met The Peterborough United Legend a few times over the years; he used to play in my dad's memorial golf day each year, and so we were on a loose kind of 'Hello, how are you?' basis. I was able to strike up a conversation with him in the hospitality bar during halftime of a Posh game one afternoon. This was largely due to him vaguely knowing who I was and my absurdly large and useless knowledge of football. Charles had sauntered off to talk to someone and left me on my own with the Legend. The conversation started with me asking him if he knew that one of his former goalkeepers was playing against Arsenal this particular day.

The Legend asked me what I was doing with myself; I said I was at college. He asked if I had a girlfriend; I said she was a pain in the arse and it was complicated! Then there was a lull of about five seconds in the conversation as The Peterborough United Legend leaned forward and bounced on his feet. He brought his hands forward and then did a sort of 'Locomotion Dance' as he built up the courage to ask, 'And . . . Er . . .' (more locomotion motions) 'You're a bit disabled, aren't you?'

So I said, 'Yes, just a bit!'

He seemed to be thinking of something to say to comfort me, and after a few moments he decided on the way to go: 'Yeah, well mate, you do your hair really nice!' The Legend seemed to talk as much with his hands as he did with his mouth, and as he comforted me he imitated how he thought I'd do my hair. I watched the second half with him in a executive box, and although the game fades in my memory, my exchange with The Peterborough United Legend is still as fresh in my mind as ever.

It is my great pleasure to anoint one of Peterborough United Football Club's finest with the honour of being first runner up in this distinguished contest. And I hope he will find some solace in my declaration that his line was the funniest out of the three.

Number one:
The winner's name is Heather, and in one fabled moment, now encrusted in gold like nostalgia and ego-soothed pride, I did love her. I met her in the student guild at Adam McGeever's university on a great night out; you could tell it was a good

night because Adam was dancing, a true indicator of the buoyancy levels being high. Others around us seemed to be having a great time; Adam's newly acquired stalker, who took on the codename 'Belly the Elephant', was immersing herself in the joy of shadowing him everywhere.

One of Adam's friends turned to me on the dance floor as a Busted song was being played and said, 'Have you pulled yet?' My reply was, predictably, 'No!' He then turned me round and ushered me to a blonde, buxom young student. After introductions and a dance floor embrace, we talked, and she said:

> 'Why are you shaking?'
> 'Oh, I'm so nervous because you're so beautiful!' Come on, it's not that bad for a thinking-on-your-feet moment!
> 'No, really, why are you shaking?' Trust me to get a low-on-confidence girl who couldn't take a compliment.
> So I changed tack: 'I sort of have a condition.'
> She looked very confused by this, and I realised I had been too vague. I came clean.
> 'I'm disabled' I confessed.

She pulled back to regard me, and this is when I fell in love with her for a moment as she proclaimed, 'You're too fit to be disabled!'

I then kissed her, partly because of what she had said and partly to end the conversation!

Our relationship lasted less than five minutes, but she will always have a spot in my heart. I will always laugh at the sheer absurdity of the statement. Disabled people are not just stereotypically drooling, wheelchair-bound beings. We come in many forms.

I admit this is a rather self-indulgent winner of the top one-line reactions to my disability, but it always brings a beaming smile to my face when I think of her statement. Our conversation came at a time in my life where I didn't exude confidence, and Heather gave my self-esteem a boost. I think that the statement has unintentional comedy and generalisation in it and that therefore qualifies it for top spot. Another element that gives Heather the edge over Mrs 'Good for You' and the Peterborough United Legend is that her words stayed with me, and I did enjoy a little purple patch with the ladies after her words of endorsement.

During my life, people have reacted in many different ways to my disability. Some reactions have been good and some have been bad. Connecting with people is about reactions to one another, and all you can do is go is take each one as it comes and then look back with an open mind and see how you feel. The three instances I've talked about here range from the rude and perplexing to the purely comical and on to the best chat-up line ever. They didn't take long to process and laugh about; sometimes it takes longer, but reactions to one's disability can produce the funniest moments you will ever come across, so don't shrug them off, keep them with you.

25

A Dentist Drill Changed My Life and That's the 'Hole' Truth

In the summer of 1998, the doctors in the oral surgery department of Peterborough District Hospital drilled into one of my healthy teeth when I was having another removed. This led to a whole chain of events that were life defining.

A few months later, my dentist discovered the results of the surgeon's less-than-accurate Black and Decker work and advised that my family and I seek out legal counsel. How exciting! Me pursuing a compensation claim: this was before the 'Where There's a Blame There's a Claim' era—before everyone started suing everyone who had dared to breathe bad breath on them. When Mum and Dad went to see the solicitor, it turned out that the case wouldn't be worth proceeding with because after the legal costs had been taken out we would hardly have enough to buy a pack of polo mints.

However, on the way out of the solicitors' office my mum turned round and uttered the words, 'It's funny; we could have been here sixteen years ago discussing a case for the negligent care Stuart received at birth!' This aroused the ever-opportunistic nature that lurks in all solicitors—some call it an ambulance-chasing mentality. The solicitor's ears pricked up as his interest was spiked. Next thing my parents knew, they were being ushered back into the office to elaborate.

My parents briefly explained the circumstances of my birth and that two doctors had told Mum and Dad that if they wanted to sue they would have a good case. My parents had decided not to pursue the claim because they felt it would take up too much of their time. They felt their efforts could better be utilised concentrating on making me as functional in this world as possible. My parents had been rewarded for their decision by seeing me surpass everyone's expectations: I walked, talked, went to mainstream school, and had done a whole lot of 'impossible' things. My mum and dad thought that the opportunity of taking legal action had gone the same way as the doctors' predictions.

The solicitor changed everything with his next words: It wasn't too late. There was a new law where the child who had received negligent care from the NHS could decide to sue when he or she reached the age of eighteen. The news was intriguing with a dab of exciting, but in no way did it feel like a reprieve. My parents had never regretted their decision not to pursue a claim, however, the solicitor had now pulled back the overhanging branches and plants to present a different route that led to somewhere none of us had imagined. I wouldn't call that place Eden—it was more a secret garden.

By the time my eighteenth birthday rolled around, the playing staff had changed. The solicitor had now been transferred to the opposing team. The law firm that my parents had first visited had imitated the actions of the Italians in the Second World War and changed sides. They now represented the NHS. The other thing that changed the state of play was that Dad had died, which left a big hole for us in many ways. He would have been such a rock for all of us during the court case, but also he was an important source of information that we now didn't have. He did not witness the negligence at my birth, but he had a vast knowledge of how my disability affected the life we led.

Although the Peterborough-based solicitors had decamped to the other side, the man we met was kind enough to point Mum and I towards a law firm that was based in Cambridge. An appointment was made, and we saw a solicitor called Sarah. What struck me was how gorgeous she was; she could have told me I had no case and I wouldn't really have taken it in because my horny eighteen-year-old mind was floating away on thoughts that were less than pure. However, I did take in enough of what she said to discern that she had agreed to handle my case.

Sarah also concluded that I was in possession of all my mental faculties, which meant that I was able to control the case rather than someone else making all decisions for me. Furthermore, because I was in such a position, there would be a five-year deadline placed on the case. If the deadline wasn't met, then the case died, which sounded scary, but it is a far better option than having an open deadline. Time is a great motivator; from just my own experience I know that if the cut-off point is coming up quickly, I am more inclined to work hard to finish the task in hand. But if I have an open deadline, I can have a tendency to put the task on the backburner. I think to myself *I can't be bothered to do that today. It will keep till tomorrow.* This book isn't about advice, but if you are suing a health authority for negligence, pushing for a five-year deadline will give your legal team a certain amount of impetus to keep the case moving forward.

Not much happened for a long time after the first meeting. We got the occasional letter predicting the size of the compensation claim: it was estimated between 750,000 and 2,500,000 pounds. Having such letters and then periods that felt so inactive, it was hard not to dream about what a difference winning the court case would make to life, especially when such large figures were being bandied about. The sums of money being talked about were more than I ever imagined, and having no concept of money and how much you need to live, I dreamt of sports cars and big white mansions. But I was a teenager and that was natural.

After the law firm and I shook hands, and the party got going, it just so happened that the NHS lost their invitation to the dance. They misplaced several important components of my medical records that would have served as damning evidence, such as the printout of the heart monitor from when Mum was in labour. This made it harder to prove when I stopped breathing. Convenient that, isn't it? But that was the kind of tactics the NHS was going to use to fight us; they did not mind getting their hands a bit dirty.

Mum found the court case really hard going. The witness statement she had to write was particularly difficult for her. She was the only witness to the birth that we had, which put an incredible amount of pressure on her. It was such a heavy weight for Mum to carry by herself. No one could make reliving that experience any easier for her, and it was unfortunate that that was the crux of the case. Mum was, as the lawyers on television would say, the 'star witness', and therefore she was very central to the case. Mum had to remember every little detail about my birth, which put her under a lot of stress. I admire how she was able to handle such pressures. For me, my future was being determined, but for Mum, her past was what was determining it.

In addition to being burdened with being the only witness to my birth, Mum did not have Dad to help her remember things about raising me. It is so much easier when you have another voice chiming in with 'Do you remember when this happened?' or 'I remember this.' Mum and I were unable to tap into Dad's memory banks, which meant that regarding the care I was given as a child, Mum had to rise to the occasion again. A lot of the time, Mum had to remember things that were very painful, and it must have been very hard not having Dad to share the load.

For a long time the court case was a hulking shadow in the background that would occasionally tap Mum and I on the shoulder. We had to submit statements about my life and how the cerebral palsy affected me on a day-to-day basis. People such as my learning support assistant from secondary school and a work colleague had to write accounts of how my cerebral palsy restricted me. However, as the world entered 2004, the court case seemed to leap out from relative obscurity and take a more active role in our lives. It was like a background character in a TV series who is suddenly brought to centre screen by a developing storyline.

The court case was in its fourth year, and it was impossible to ignore its presence. Life went on, but we seemed to be hampered by partial paralysis. For example, Mum wanted to sell the cleaning business, but she was keeping hold of it until we knew the outcome of the case. If we lost, I would need an income and the business provided that, but if we won there would be more options available to us.

The solicitors advised us to go away and leave them to think about the court case, which was easier in the beginning, but when the case really started snowballing, it became the 'hit song of the moment' that wouldn't get out of our heads. The more momentum that the case generated, the more specialists I saw. The selected expects were sometimes enlisted by the defence and sometimes by the prosecution.

I was assessed by various doctors, a psychologist, an occupational therapist, and more that I have forgotten. I had to travel to different places in the country to have various examinations. Sometimes the reports would be interesting, and other times depressing. It was hard to keep focussed on having a glass-half-empty stance. The worse the report the better it was for the case, but having my life taken apart really weighed down on me. I was an insecure person anyway, so to see my fears being written about by professionals gave them a bigger sense of reality. My ego and self-esteem took some hammer blows during the case. Never was this more so than in the December of 2004.

On December 22, 2004, the weather was dingy and damp; whenever I remember the day, I remember the pavement. The concrete had had no choice but to take in the unwanted refugees—raindrops—earlier in the day and now the colour underfoot was a collage of brown, grey, and black. Adam McGeever called me, and I stepped out of the bookies where I was having a tea break to take the call.

> 'You're on the front page of the *ET*!'
> 'Yeah, right! What the fuck for?'
> 'About the court case. They've said stuff about you having problems with satisfying women!'
> 'I'll call you back!'

I put the phone back in my pocket and spun round on my feet. The newsagent shop was only a fifteen-second walk away, but nonetheless I sprinted to the shop. I burst through the door and snapped up a newspaper just as if I was pulling a child out of a road with a speeding vehicle approaching. I slung my money on to the counter and dropped the change twice when it was given back to me. I got outside; I was standing still but my hands behaved as if they were signalling a plane for take-off. I looked like I was having a fit as my eyes darted around after the newspaper that my hands wouldn't keep still. My heart was racing as I tried to scan the front page. At first I couldn't see the story; my eyes were scurrying across the page too fast and all I could see was an article about group of idiots who were trying to stir up a melee as they had been turned away from a club because they were dressed as Santa. Then my eyes came to rest in the bottom right-hand corner, fucking bastards!

I read the article with shock turning into disbelief and then into a white-hot rage. I couldn't believe that I would have made the front page, but when I read it I saw that nothing sells better than sex, lies, and money. The article was a riddled with inaccuracies and lies.

The article screamed my 'reasons' for suing at the top of its voice. 'Stuart Maloney now believes his prospects of marriage or having a stable relationship with a partner have been reduced by his disability.' Granted, I have had trouble with my disability and women, but that wasn't my reason for suing; if that was the case, surely ugly people would be suing their parents for giving them bad genes. The writ that was served on my behalf had one sentence in it that said that I may have problems with relationships, but in the grand scheme of things it was a footnote. The reason I was suing was because the hospital's negligence had led to me suffering irreversible brain damage that affected my whole life, not that I just couldn't get laid.

The article made quite a lot of mistakes. The journalist attested that I 'did not breathe for twelve minutes', which if that were true the title of this book would carry significantly less weight. They said that I was delivered with the umbilical cord wrapped around my 'head' rather than my neck, and the article also failed to mention that I had pulled the placenta away, which affected my oxygen supply. In all, I was deprived of the required amount of oxygen for just under an hour before being born, which means that stating twelve minutes is quite a glaring error.

I hated the *Evening Telegraph* for running the story, but now I am able to see that the article was a result of absolutely appalling journalism and awful editing. But more than that, the *ET* had been used as a pawn by the defence. My distorted story had been leaked to the press with the intention of humiliating me into dropping the case. The *Evening Telegraph* was manipulated into portraying me as a person who—although my 'intellect was not damaged' and I had a 'successful job'—still wanted my piece of the pie.

My Christmas was ruined. I had spent four years keeping the court case a relative secret, but in one day that all was knocked down with a wrecking ball that hung on a string of lies. People at work who had never spoken to me before started talking to me, and people stared at me for a while. But what the defence didn't seem to realise was that when a man's sexual abilities or dating capabilities are held up for public perusal, there is really not that much more pain you can inflict upon him. I just thought if I gave up, I would have been humiliated for nothing, and so we marched on.

The court case was always at a crossroads it seemed; it was either on the brink of collapse or completely solid with no chance of losing. There was no in-between. It would stall and then it would spurt along. We went through a string of lawyers; it seemed that when the bosses saw the case and picked up the scent of cash in the air, the big guns were brought in. Then a big gun would leave; at one point we had a doctor in charge of the case! I thought at the time, *Why in the world do I have a doctor instead of a solicitor running my case?*

The last solicitor seemed to push the case forward more than any of the previous three. In fact, she pushed the case right along with her to another law firm. As we followed the yellow brick road towards trial, my legal team imparted upon Mum and I that the venue in which the respective sides would don wigs and cross legal pads was going to be the Old Bailey. After hearing that sentence, Mum and I felt as if we had been led into the wolves den. It all seemed very scary when we thought about the sharp teeth being shown by the wild dogs.

We had been told that we were going to be in the big leagues, and knowing that there was no room for error became very daunting. I would have a butterfly flutter over my heart whenever I contemplated my history being written in such a historic place, but the thoughts didn't consume me. Mum, however, was different. She could be put on the stand to talk about the birth, and with that constantly tap dancing on her mind, her emotions blew around her body like a hurricane. *What will happen? What if I make a mistake?* Mum asked herself such questions. She dreaded the fine-combing of my delivery that was set to take place. The nerves and emotions shooed her towards nights of little sleep and constant worry.

February 11, 2005, was the day my family went to see *Mary Poppins the Musical*; Simone had been given four tickets as a Christmas present. Mum, Charles, Simone, and I set off for London to watch the matinee performance. It was okay from my point of view, a good stage set, but half of the original songs were missing, which took away some of the magic. When we got out of the theatre, Mum looked at her phone and saw that she had eight missed calls from my solicitor.

Mum rang her back and was told that the NHS had offered to settle for one million pounds! Wow! One million! We were told to think about it and then come to London on the Monday for a meeting to give my team of barristers and lawyers a decision. I think Mum and I were pretty much decided upon settling from the moment we heard the offer. Mum had no more to give, and I looked upon myself as being quite a poor gambler, thus I did not want to push my luck when we had a good offer on the table. I wanted to cash in my chips and get out of the casino.

Three days later, Mum and I set out to listen to the advice that would be given, but we were sure what our stance would be. The meeting was rather laid back, and although the younger and more ambitious solicitors wanted to push for one point one million, my senior barrister was happy that I had decided to accept the offer. That sealed it really; if the most experienced member of the team thought I should settle then it was clear to us that I should take the money and walk away. The funny thing was that when my barrister rang the defence to tell them I had decided to accept their offer, they said, 'Oh, well we thought we had a good case anyway!' Okay, why offer to settle then?

And there you have it! The hourglass had still a few grains left in the top before the five years ran out when I walked out of the law courts with a million-pound settlement. I can still feel the relief in my stomach as I write about it. When the crisp winter wind hit my face, it was like someone shouting 'Hey, this is a new beginning!' We were living out a movie scene where fists punching the air and high fives would not have been out of place. We were walking on air for days afterwards. We had done it. We had righted a wrong, and in doing so, I had financial security.

It was a glorious time; if there was a time to move on and put the past behind us, this was it. The common conversation in our family was about looking for my house and working out how to manage my money. Now financial dealings, bank accounts, investments, and the like are a part of my life that does not really faze me, but when these topics of conversation were first broached they were completely foreign to me. There was a duel carriageway built above me, and a lot of what my new financial advisor was saying was driving along it over my head.

When a spy has just finished a mission, he can be at his most vulnerable because he can let his guard down. The spy in his euphoric mood thinks that nothing can hurt him now, he's out of the field and safe, but that is when enemies can strike. The same thing happened with Mum and me. We thought that people would be happy and understand what our achievement meant, but as it turned out, there were jealous eyes making plans for themselves.

Two members of my mum's family wanted to purchase the cleaning company from us, and when that didn't come to pass, they became very bitter. Their attitude was summed up when they staked their claim for the business by saying, 'Stuart and Josie have had all this luck; they should really spread it around'. I will always be hurt by this comment. I didn't feel lucky in the slightest to have sued the NHS.

I was relieved that everything had worked out and it was over, but I would have much rather not have been subjected to negligent care as a child. But that is the way the cards had been dealt. It wasn't a lottery win; my money is a combination of damages and loss of income. I turn cold thinking about those ignorant words that slap my family in the face. There is no luck in being disabled, and maybe if they had taken a step back they would have realised that, but they just didn't get it. They were corrupted by greed and jealousy, which is very sad.

I find it somewhat ironic that a petty mistake during a routine oral surgery procedure led my family and I back to the massive mistake that took place when I was born. Talk about the medical profession shooting themselves in the foot! It was a long journey, and I have a lot of people to thank, but none more so than the clumsy oral surgeon who drilled into my healthy tooth: without him, I would never have taken this path.

26

THE THREE-LEGGED DOG

A dog walks without his lead in front of his owner. He looks content as he saunters along the walking path that punctuates the landscape of the national park like a spellcheck. The dog sniffs a tree and he goes to the toilet. He barks at a fellow dog and is scolded by its owner before they carry on their walk. But when you look a bit closer you realise that the dog is missing a leg. It seems bizarre that a dog can be hampered in such a way and yet be so active and appear so happy. But here is a thought: *A three-legged dog is still a dog*. The dog had adapted to having three legs instead of four, and he could still do all the tasks that he wanted to do such as walking, barking, sniffing, and the usual dog stuff.

When I was young, Dad talked to me about the brain damage I suffered when I was born. I knew that being deprived of oxygen for nearly an hour and being stillborn for twenty-six minutes had caused the brain damage and hence the cerebral palsy. I wanted to know what part of my brain had been damaged and what it would have been doing if it wasn't damaged.

Dad wasn't a scientist, but he answered my questions the best he could. I asked him to explain how my brain functioned with a part of it that was basically dead. Dad told me that because my brain had been damaged at birth, it had never had access to that area, which meant it just adapted and worked around the problem in order to provide good brain function. I was amazed by the story. The idea that the brain can be productive like factory workers who have to cover for a colleague who doesn't turn up for a shift still is extraordinary to me. Especially as I struggle to adapt to predictive texting!

I duly forgot the discussion about my brain damage—as one does when one has brain damage!—and childhood gave way to adulthood. One day I was watching a documentary about dwarves. When exploring the life of a primordial dwarf, which is a rare type of dwarfism that leads to the person being very small—even for a dwarf—at every stage of life, the program came to the subject of intellect and brain function. Because primordial dwarves are small in every respect, including internal organs, they have a smaller brain, and they are sometimes born without the part of the brain in charge of intellect.

The narrator said however, that if the damage or absence of a part of the brain happens at an early enough stage of life, then the brain can reroute the signals and other parts of the brain can perform the tasks that the affected part of the brain would have been responsible for. I travelled back to the time that Dad described my brain trauma, and I realised that it wasn't just my dad's amateur diagnosis of what had happened. My dad must have read up on the workings of the brain. I actually find just the thought of that subject to be very intimidating. Out of curiosity, I decided to follow suit using the Internet. This is what I found:

Scientists have shown that after diffuse axonal injury, neurons can spontaneously adapt and recover by sprouting some of the remaining healthy fibres of the neuron into the spaces once occupied by the degenerated axon. These fibres can develop in such a way that the neuron can resume communication with neighbouring neurons.

I was amazed all over again, and then on the way to London, my repaired neurons designed a metaphor to describe the adaptation of the brain that took place in my head shortly after I was born: my brain is a three-legged dog! It adapted to life without what was thought to be an essential part, and now leads a life where it performs normal tasks with as much ease as possible.

When observing a three-legged dog or a person with a disability, one can be overcome with a sense of pity. The onlooker feels as if the subject of their attention has lost something, but that is not always the case. Beyond the fact that I never had the part of my brain that is damaged, I now do not feel as if I have lost out. My brain and my life have been enriched by the alternative paths that my neurons have taken. Until I looked upon myself as a three-legged dog, I didn't fully comprehend how active and highly functioning I am. I broke down life and I saw how much I actually do. My story has had many triumphs, and that makes me happy. As an adult, I now do not wish for my 'fourth leg'. Recently somebody suggested to me that going in an oxygen chamber could reduce my symptoms almost to the point of curing them. I felt repulsed by the thought. I smiled and nodded, but once I was away from the well-intentioned person, I said, 'Some people do not want a cure; they are happy as they are'. That point seems to highlight that a three-legged dog is a beautiful creature, not something worthy of pity.

We are now at the end of my twenty-six years, and the destination that I have reached is a final sense of acceptance. I will always be, and I am very proud to be, a three-legged dog.

THE LAST WORD

I wrote that I am a three-legged dog, but I could argue that I have other animals inside of me. In Japanese legends, the koi fish represents different things, one being strength in times of adversity. The koi is known for swimming upstream, and the Japanese believe that this symbolises persistence and willingness to carry on even though it may be swept away. Like the koi, I have surpassed expectations by overcoming various obstacles that have been put in front of me in my life; I am still here.

I believe that even at my birth I had an ingrained battling spirit that would not let me give up. There is no greater adversity than being dead, especially when you are a newborn. Obviously, the doctors and nurses who resuscitated me have to take a lot of the credit, but I believe I could have easily been swept away by the circumstances surrounding my delivery; I wasn't. I started swimming upstream, and I have never stopped since.

A seed was planted in that delivery room on April 10, 1982—a sort of siege mentality that I took with me everywhere. I kept this aura around me, and my parents nurtured it. The whole concept seems so natural to me that I don't even think about it. If I am ill, I just carry on; if I cannot do something around the house, I do not give in until I find a solution one way or the other. I have had times where the only thread that has kept my life together has been this instinct to fight.

This spirit of not giving in leads me to think I may have a spider or two creeping around inside of me, as horrible as that may sound. I don't just mean because research suggests we swallow spiders in our sleep; I mean that I identify with the eight-legged creature from the fable *The King and the Spider*. The story was written about Robert the Bruce, who as king of Scotland had been beaten in six battles by the English. One night he sat and watched a spider struggle to fix the strands of her web to the wooden rafter above his head. The spider failed each time it tried, but never did it give up. On the spider's seventh attempt, she succeeded in joining her web together, and this is supposed to have inspired the Bruce to fight on. My life has been the web: I may fail time after time, but I will keep trying until I succeed.

To write this book I have had to look deep inside myself, and as a consequence, the kind of story that has been told has at times been deeply introspective and self-analytical. To dig so far down inside wasn't my original intention; I just wanted to tell my story with a few anecdotes thrown in along the way. But I am not complaining, because I feel that by picking scabs and letting my emotions run across the page to mix with my tears of laughter and sadness, the story has taken on more layers. I have been able to make sense of different aspects of my life that I didn't even know needed making sense of. I hope that, in some way, my personal story has resonated with you, and I will be very happy if it has inspired young people with disabilities or even given them some understanding of what they are going through.

I have several tattoos that map out my journey to date. I feel a deep, symbolic connection with each one. As I look at the number twenty-six spelt out in Roman numerals on the top of my arm every day, I am reminded where my life started and that I am lucky to be here. I have a tattoo of a hand letting go of a balloon, which not only reminds me of outliving the life expectancy I talked about in the chapter titled Sixteen Balloons, but it also is a constant reminder to let go of things in my life. We all have scars, and I will never forget the hurtful experiences in my life, but writing this book has allowed me to let go of a lot of the pain I felt about them.

The scars that we pick up along the way shape us like carpenters' tools. Hopefully we can learn from our experiences or find meaning and move on. I found my life policy when I died at birth, and every day I try to live my life in accordance with words that I wrote and had tattooed on me so I don't forget them:

> *Forever my spirit breathes from within*
> *Never will it leave or give in.*

ABOUT THE AUTHOR

Stuart Maloney was born April 10, 1982. Stuart was deprived of oxygen when he was born and suffered brain damage. At eighteen months of age, he was diagnosed with cerebral palsy.

Stuart was not supposed to live very long, but with the help of a loving family and a courageous spirit, he overcame many obstacles to make it to adulthood.

At the age of twenty-two, Stuart successfully sued the National Health Service for the negligent care he received at his birth. The case was settled out of court.

Stuart lives in Peterborough and runs his own cleaning business. He is a qualified cycling coach and teaches adaptive cycling to people with disabilities.

Through his writing, Stuart aspires to tackle the stigma of disability and show that people with disabilities can live full lives. The story of his journey, *26,* is his first book.

Lightning Source UK Ltd.
Milton Keynes UK
UKOW051214211111